LAW AND ETHICS IN COUNSELING

LAW AND ETHICS IN COUNSELING

Dean L. Hummel

Lou C. Talbutt

M. David Alexander

Virginia Polytechnic Institute
and State University
Blacksburg, Virginia

VAN NOSTRAND REINHOLD COMPANY

Library of Congress Catalog Card Number: 84-13139
ISBN: 0-442-23384-1

Manufactured in the United States of America.

Published by Van Nostrand Reinhold Company Inc.
135 West 50th Street
New York, New York 10020

Van Nostrand Reinhold Company Limited
Molly Millars Lane
Wokingham, Berkshire RG11 2PY, England

Van Nostrand Reinhold
480 Latrobe Street
Melbourne, Victoria 3000, Australia

Macmillan of Canada
Division of Gage Publishing Limited
164 Commander Boulevard
Agincourt, Ontario MIS 3C7, Canada

15 14 13 12 11 10 9 8 7 6 5 4 3 2 1

Library of Congress Cataloging in Publication Data
Hummel, Deal L.
Law and ethics in counseling.
Includes index.
1. Student counselors—Legal status, laws, etc.—United States. 2. Counseling ethics. 3. Counseling—Law and legislation—United States. I. Talbutt, Lou. II. Alexander, M. David. III. Title.
KF4192.5.G8H85 1984 174'.3'0973 84-13139
ISBN 0-442-23384-1

CONTENTS

PREFACE

This book resulted from professional colleagues' requests from our more than 60 accumulated years of experience in the helping professions, and from an obvious need for a contemporary and comprehensive work in law and ethics for counselors. As recently as 5 years ago, Robert Callis, in *The Status of Guidance and Counseling in the Nation's Schools* (American Personnel and Guidance Association, 1979), urged that "immediate action needs to be taken to eradicate the deficiency in knowledge by practicing counselors and counselor educators of the law and ethics of counseling and guidance" (p. 206). We have attempted in this book to write a course text and a desk top reference that will fill a void in the professional field of practicing counselors and in the classroom of counselor training programs.

The first book dealing extensively with legal aspects of counseling was *Law of Guidance and Counseling,* edited by M. H. Ware (W. H. Anderson Co., Cincinnati, 1964). A variety of works, reports, and journal articles have appeared during the last decade, but few have attempted to fuse the many-faceted aspects of law and ethics in a single volume. Since 1964, numerous laws affecting counseling, scores of court cases, hundreds of regulations, and changes in ethical standards for counselors have made an impact on the counseling profession. We undertook this project as a professional contribution, and we traveled the stacks of legal and educational libraries because of our strong belief that the helping professions needed this volume.

Throughout this book, legal references are cited according to the *Publication Manual of the American Psychological Association,* 3rd edition, 1983. Legal references differ from other kinds of materials. However, the citations are formed in a similar manner and enable the reader to locate the name of the statute or court case, name of volume, volume number, and page(s) of the reference.

Much of the content of this book has application to the wide variety of client contacts and problems encountered by professionals in the helping professions and to those whose major helping approaches involves counseling. We have, however, emphasized ethics and laws applicable to student, parent, and school counseling.

We wish to acknowledge the long-term support of counseling students, practicing professional counselors, state educational offices, and university trainers during our years of service to the profession. We are indebted to the various professional associations, especially the American Association for Counseling and Development, for permission to reproduce their materials.

We also relied upon our experiences as professional counselors, educators, and legal consultants as we selected material to be included. We trust that our judgments, our research, and our professional dedication will provide readers with a helpful and authoritative guide to their legal and ethical lives.

DEAN L. HUMMEL
LOU C. TALBUTT
M. DAVID ALEXANDER

LAW AND ETHICS IN COUNSELING

Part I

THE FUNCTIONING PROFESSIONAL

Chapter 1

The Counseling Profession

AN EMERGING PROFESSION

Within this century the profession of counseling has developed and grown as an important and necessary helping process. It assists individuals with personal development, career and life-style planning, decision making, and resolution of behavior problems (Talbutt and Hummel, 1982). Counselors are found in public and private schools, institutions of higher education, social agencies, business and industry, and private practice. Counseling is now performed by a variety of persons with a diversity of training and with or without affiliation with professional associations. "Counseling is a major social force and has a profound influence not only on the lives of individuals, but upon public beliefs and public policy as well" (Van Hoose, 1980, 1).

This emerging profession can be traced in history and in theory to a wide variety of services designed to help human beings achieve survival and happiness in their life activities. Historically Freud developed a method (psycholoanalysis) to treat mentally ill patients (Mora, 1975), thereby promoting the science of psychology in helping to cure human maladies. Clifford Beers, in *A Mind That Found Itself* (1956, originally published in 1909), gave impetus to the helping professions by being a founder in mental hygiene and in social work. Frank Parsons, in his book *Choosing a Vocation* (1967, originally published in 1909), gave rise to the vocational guidance movement and to counseling in the schools. Behaviorism—through the work of Watson,

Skinner, and others—stimulated the use of measurement in behavior counseling. In his struggle with psychiatry and behaviorism, Rogers (1974) led a humanistic movement with his client-centered counseling and psychotherapy, and Ellis in *Reason and Emotion in Psychotherapy* (1962) introduced a cognitive-behavior approach through "rational emotive therapy."

To the above twentieth-century historical and theoretical items could be added the preprofessional work in helping methods for troubled and striving persons. And to the origins of the pioneering and creative work of analysists, behaviorists, and humanists could be added at least sixty different labeled approaches (theories) used in the helping professions. To these approaches could be added countless variations, used by special counselors working in special settings with specially defined clients. Indeed, it can be conjectured that there are as many approaches as there are counselors, for a labeled counseling approach translated into a helping process takes into account the unique characteristics of counselors and clients, the setting in which the process takes place, the particular client problem, and the total environment in which the client functions.

Counseling as an emerging helping profession has become a major human service enterprise during this century in the United States and abroad. According to the *Occupational Outlook Quarterly* (spring, 1980), various types of counselors in the United States numbered 976,100, including 5,000 college career planning and placement counselors, 6,100 employment counselors, 252,000 pastoral counselors, 130,000 counseling psychologists, 19,000 rehabilitation counselors, 45,000 school counselors, 385,000 social workers, and 134,000 social service aides. Marriage and family counselors, school psychologists, mental health counselors, health and recreation counselors, retirement counselors, and a variety of other helping professional personnel would raise the total to well over 2 million. In 1975 Belkin commented, "The profession of counseling is a relatively recent development still in its flowering stages" (p. 1).

COUNSELOR ROLE AND CONTROL

Basic criteria of a profession are that membership roles and control of services are established. These criteria suggest that standards for professional entry, training, ethics, and relationships with consumers of service and among member professionals are established. The criteria also imply the establishment of procedures and requirements for licensing or certification (Van Hoose and Kottler, 1977). As in law and medicine, professionals can be regulated, held accountable, and disciplined by state and federal statue and case law. Because of the diversity of types of counselors and the services provided by the helping professions, role and control are less than exact or standard in practice. However, law and the major established professional associations have adopted training standards, role definitions, and ethical procedures that tend to be the guidelines for all practitioners in the helping professions.

The American Association for Counseling and Development (AACD) (formerly American Personnel and Guidance Association [APGA]), and the American Psychological Association (APA) have in the past two decades taken the lead in establishing role and control for services provided by their membership. The *Ethical Standards* (1981) of AACD (APGA) and "Ethical Principles of Psychologists" (1981) tend to be viewed as guidelines for most professionals in counseling. The implications of these standards will be dealt with in more detail in chapter 2.

PROFESSIONAL MATURITY

Criteria for determining professional maturity are generally agreed upon (Dunlop, 1968; McCully, 1963). These criteria stipulate that the professional group and its members "(1) can clearly define their role, (2) offer unique services, (3) possess special knowledge and skills, (4) have an explicit code of ethics, (5) have the [legal] right to offer the service as a profession describes it, and (6) have the ability to monitor the practice of the professions" (Nugent, 1981, 40). In varying degrees the counseling "profession" has subscribed to these criteria. However, the wide variety of types of counselors and their work settings are presenting a continuing challenge to the development of professional maturity.

Because of the interpersonal nature of the counseling process, the maturity factor rests primarily with the individual counselor. The helping professions, perhaps more than any other, carry the responsibility for both professional and personal maturity.

THE INFLUENCE OF PSYCHOLOGY AND PSYCHOANALYSIS

In classic philosophy, apart from religious philosophy, essential ideas relating to maturity seemed to have included (*a*) a transcendental conception of meaning more or less independent of immediate, contemporary events, (*b*) an understanding of contemporary events beyond, or below, surface manifestation, (*c*) acceptance of the conditions of human tragedy as inescapable fate, and (*d*) a belief that mature behavior results from a reasoned and courageous course of conduct in the face of unavoidable decisions.

In the growth of philosophy as a discipline, a continuous philosophical quest has been pursued by thinkers of all persuasions right up to the present day in attempts to know through analysis and reason the nature of the right and of good (Smith and Debbins, 1945). All this philosophizing has been a clear reflection of humanity's unquenchable aspiration to know the right and the good and to do it. We could stretch our thesis a bit here and there and say this long history of philosophizing has been an index of humanity's striving to become "mature."

Beyond reason and the intellectual pursuits of philosophy has been the faith of religion as expressing a reality of man's psyche. Thus, to philosophical conceptions of maturity have been added, from religion, ideas of humility, compassion, love. These ideas have been taken over by modern counseling practice, confirmed in clinical findings, and expressed in phrases like the following from William C. Menninger in talking about "yardsticks" of maturity: "The capacity to love [is the] most important of all, the underlying base of good mental health and the only neutralizer of hostilities." (Menninger, 1954, 24).

With the advent of formal psychology with Wundt and his laboratory and the beginning of psychoanalysis with Freud, the scene shifted from a preoccupation with ideas to a systematic study of human beings. In those beginnings, we have twin radical conceptions (still revolutionary):

1. The psychological contents and processes can be systematically studied, analyzed, described, and classified.
2. Outside influences can be exerted upon psychological contents and processes to produce differential and predicatable objective consequences.

Yet there has persisted the indomitable and inextinguishable belief that something in the person remains beyond analysis, beyond ordinary environmental influence, and beyond prediction. Psychology has not succeeded in doing away with either philosophy or religion. Thus, philosophers like F. S. C. Northrup have been able to declare that the cognitive, reasoning, analytical, and scientific aspect of a person is only half of the truth, that beneath this conscious overlay is the affective, irrational, meditative, and artistic aspect—the two making up the totality of one's being (Northrup, 1946). Not only were certain philosophers maintaining this belief, but psychologists such as Carl Jung and Gordon Allport were also providing similar testimony. Allport (1961) declared that

> an exclusively psychological conception of the human person is a vain dream. One must know also his metaphysical nature and his place in the cosmic design. Ancient wisdom, both philosophical and theological, should be consulted and incorporated lest we find ourselves dealing with elaborate trivalities. Psychology is a recent arrival on the scene, and its new insights are as best partial. (P. 1)

Table 1-1. Categories of Criteria of Psychological Maturity

1. *Relations to Reality*
   Ability to deal constructively with reality
   Correct perception of world and self
   Effective organization of work toward goals
   Capacity to learn and profit from experience
   Outer-centered interests
   Industry and competence
   Ability to accept frustrations
   Creativeness
   Planfulness
2. *Relations to Others*
   Social responsibility
   Social feeling
   Acceptance of others
   Relating consistently to people with mutual satisfaction and helpfulness
   Dependability, responsibility, tolerance, truthfulness, open-mindedness
   Freedom from prejudice
3. *Relations to Self or within the Self*
   Sense of self-identity and autonomy
   Unity of personality
   Self-reliance
   Character and integrity in the ethical sense
   Ability to criticize self
   Self-objectification
   Self-confidence
4. *Relations to Conceptions of Value and Meaning*
   Achievement of meaning and responsibility
   Unifying philosophy of life

A study of available literature bearing directly upon conceptions of psychological maturity reveals a preoccupation with criteria of maturity in the form of trait formulations—"social responsibility," "dependability," "correct perception of reality," and "acceptance of self"—and behaviors associated with designated developmental stages, such as "hetrosexual interests," "active peer relationships," "impulsive gratification." There seems to be little about the *psychological process* of maturation, especially in connection with the counseling process. A study by Mathewson (1963) revealed approximately sixty trait designations or criteria of maturity that conceivably might relate to learned responses for counseling maturity. All of these can be classified under four major categories as given in Table 1-1.

In listing criteria of maturity from the literature under the four relational categories shown in Table 1-1, we are actually presenting four major perceptions of the meaning of maturity that may be directly connected with possible counseling processes and influences.

1. *Relations to reality:* maturation as increasing competence in understanding and meeting reality, in coping with the affairs of life—personal, social, vocational
2. *Relations to others:* maturation as interpersonal development, as growth in the genuine capacity of the self to relate wholesomely and collaboratively with others and to fulfill social responsibilities
3. *Relations to self:* maturation as development in understanding, individuating, intergrating, accepting, and directing the self
4. *Relations to value and meaning:* maturation as transcedence of self and culture in an expanding appreciation of universal values and meanings

We may summarize these four conceptions as maturation for personal effectiveness, for social relationship, for self-integration and direction, and for value orientation.

Perhaps in thus abstracting and condensing the many facets of maturity and maturation we lose some of the significance and richness of the more detailed criteria previously listed, but there is an advantage for counseling and guidance in so doing. It facilitates our progress toward two important conclusions; namely, that we do not want to settle for just one or two of these pathways toward maturity but wish to incorporate all four within a complete and rounded idea of maturity and, further, that expressed in these summarized terms, we recognize goals and possible outcomes that are meaningful in the field of counseling and that we may be able to do something about.

PRIMARY AND SECONDARY COMMITMENTS

The helping professions generally declare attending to the individual's concerns and behavior to be a primary commitment. A secondary commitment to others, to institutions, and to society is, however, seen as both a legal and ethical mandate. In many situations commitment for both counselor and client becomes a matter of freedom versus responsibility.

On one hand, professionals have always striven for freedom and autonomy in developing their professional status. At the same time, social institutions have always been concerned with control of behavior. It would seem that counselors and the profession they represent, and social institutions and the consumers they represent, are basically in conflict with regard to the responsibility involved in freedom and control objectives.

Some disquieting questions are included in any discussion of the freedom versus control conflict. Control suggests control by someone or something. *Who* should control individual professional behavior? The person himself?

Perhaps the controlling forces would be some aspect of the mind or self. Such a view would not be supported by the behavioral sciences. The assumption of a fragmented view of the services would only add confusion. Neither would it be acceptable to view society as the single controlling force of individual behavior, for society is simply composed of individuals whose behavior it would be proposed to control.

The proposal sometimes made in educational and psychological conferences that computers can determine professionals' goals, that technicians decide our policies would probably be construed as the most serious of errors. For one thing, computers cannot tell us what our goals ought to be. However, in an era of confusion and anxiety, it is not surprising that technology is in fashion, sometimes justified by expressions of efficiency, objectivity, and feasibility. The danger is to tend to ask only the questions the machine can answer, to teach only the things the machine can teach, and to limit our research to the quantitative work the machine can do. Followed through to the bitter end, it takes no stretch of the imagination to predict a "1984" in which the image of humanity would be overhauled into the image of the very machine by which we study and control human beings.

As Rollo May suggests (Lloyd-Jones and Westervelt, 1963), a central distinguishing characteristic is a human being's capacity to be conscious of what he or she is experiencing, to experience himself or herself as subject and object at the same time, to be aware of having a world and being interrelated with it. Mind is the individual's capacity to transcend the immediate concrete situation and think in terms of the possible. Out of this capacity to experience a gap between self and world, between stimulus and response, the human race has developed the capacity to use symbols, to reason, and to speak. These are the mediational responses, unique to our cognitive ability for self-expression, crucial for professionals and in the counseling process.

This inseparable relation of self and world also implies *responsibility,* a term meaning "responding," "response to." One cannot become a self except as being engaged in responding to the world of which one is a part.

What seems obvious is that a person moves *toward* freedom and responsibility in functioning as she or he becomes more aware of the deterministic experiences in life. That is, a person brings to awareness those aspects of experiences that have tended to condition personal development. As an individual explores and understands experiences of rejection or love, personal encounters as a minority group member, status in the searching generation to which she or he belongs, or even the struggle with the abstractions of higher education, an expanded margin of freedom is discovered. Increased awareness of the infinite deterministic forces in life brings more freedom.

Freedom, therefore, is not the opposite of determinististm. Freedom is the individual's capacity *to know that he or she is the determined one,* the pause that refreshes between stimulus and response that cues her or his behavior toward an alternative that may be chosen. To clarify the compatibility of freedom and responsibility, two principles may be extracted from this thesis. First, freedom is a quality of action resulting from the awareness of self and environmental forces. A totality of self with functional awareness is the key to freedom of action. Second, *freedom is always enmeshed with responsibility.* This principle recognizes the *limits* of freedom. Freedom is neither license nor ever simply "doing as one pleases." Behavior cued by whim or fancy denies the freedom of self to engage in quality action. Freedom is limited by the fact that a helping service exists in a society (or subsociety, such as a university) and an awareness of relationships between the service and society. These two basic principles tend to be the foundation on which role and control of the helping professions are based.

EXTERNAL CONTROLS

External controls of practice in the helping professions are numerous but in many cases vague because a definitive delineation of the various legal ramifications of counseling has not been incorporated in a national code of laws. Consumers, of course, do provide some control by their acceptance of counseling and by their acknowledged satisfaction of their participation in counseling.

Controls affecting the helping professions come primarily from two sources: (1) jurisdictional and regulatory powers over various professions practicing within individual states, and (2) national or state social legislation that provide support for counseling of some type, much of it from third-party payments.

Licensing, certification, or registration regulations for psychologists have been established in all 50 states, the District of Columbia, and 7 provinces of Canada (Fretz and Mills, 1980). On the other hand, only 6 states (Alabama, Florida, Idaho, Arkansas, Texas, and Virginia) hae enacted counselor licensing laws. And in 1983 North Carolina enacted a registration law for counselors (Bui, 1983). In 1979 New Hampshire enacted a licensing law for rehabilitation counselors (Fretz and Mills, 1980), and in 1983 all 50 states required school counselors to be certificated (Hummel and Humes, 1984). With each licensing certification or registration law, there is a statement of role and function and of ethical practice. The significance of these regulating laws is not only control of practice by professionals who qualify by law but that these laws tend to apply to counselor practice whether or not the counselor holds professional association membership or is licensed, certificated, or registered as a professional counselor (Hummel, 1980).

As suggested above, regardless of levels of preparation, institutional setting, or private practice, practitioners in the helping professions (counseling) are subject to assessment and control by law and professional counseling associations. Role statements and standards of ethics can, in effect, be viewed as "laws" of conduct. A breach of a stated code of ethics can result in litigation against a practicing counselor and/or revocation of license or association membership of a professional counselor. The following ethical standards (Virginia State Board of Professional Counselors, 1977, 17-25) are suggested as a prime example of principal guidelines for all counseling practitioners.

Section V: Ethical Standards

FOR 5.1: Code of Ethics

Professional Counselors believe in the dignity and worth of the individual. They are committed to increasing knowledge of human behavior and understanding of themselves and others. While pursuing these endeavors, they make every reasonable effort to protect the welfare of those who seek their services or of any subject that may be the object of study. They use their skills only for purposes consistent with these values and do not knowingly permit their misuse by others. While demanding for themselves freedom of inquiry and communication, professional counselors accept the responsibility this freedom confers: competence, objectivity in the application of skills and concern for the best interests of clients, colleagues, and society in general. In the pursuit of these ideals, professional counselors subscribe to the following principles:

PRINCIPLE 1. RESPONSIBILITY

In their commitment to the understanding of human behavior, professional counselors value objectivity and integrity, and in providing services they maintain the highest standards. They accept responsibility for the consequences of their work and make every effort to insure that their services are used appropriately.

a. Professional counselors accept the ultimate responsibility for selecting appropriate areas for investigation and the methods relevant to minimize the possibility that their finding will be misleading. They provide thorough discussion of the limitations of their data and alternative hypotheses, especially where their work touches on social policy or might be misconstrued to the detriment of specific age, sex, ethnic, socio-economic, or other social categories. In publishing reports of their work, they never discard observations that may modify the interpretation of results. Professional counselors take credit only for the work they have actually done. In pursuing research, professional counselors ascertain that their efforts will not lead to changes in individuals or organizations unless such changes are part of the agreement at the time of obtaining informed consent. Professional counselors clarify in advance the expectations for sharing and utilizing research data. They avoid dual relationships which may limit objectivity, whether theoretical, political, or monetary, so that interference with data, subjects, and milieu is kept to a minimum.

b. As employees of an institution or agency, professional counselors have the responsibility of remaining alert to institutional pressures which may distort reports of counseling findings or use them in ways counter to the promotion of human welfare.

c. When serving as members of governmental or other organizational bodies, professional counselors remain accountable as individuals to the Code of Ethics of the Virginia Board of Professional Counselors.

d. As teachers, professional counselors recognize their primary obligation to help others acquire knowledge and skill. They maintain high standards of scholarship and objectivity by presenting counseling information fully and accurately, and by giving appropriate recognition to alternative viewpoints.

e. As practitioners, professional counselors know that they bear a heavy social responsibility because their recommendations and professional actions may alter the lives of others. They, therefore, remain fully cognizant of their impact and alert to personal, social, organizational, financial or political situations or pressures which might lead to misuse of their influence.

f. Professional counselors provide reasonable and timely feedback to employees, trainees, supervisees, students and others whose work they may evaluate.

PRINCIPLE 2. COMPETENCE

The maintenance of high standards of professional competence is a responsibility shared by all professional counselors in the interest of the public and the profession as a whole. Professional counselors recognize the boundaries of their competence and the limitations of their techniques and only provide services, use techniques, or offer opinions as professionals that meet recognized standards. Throughout their careers, professional counselors maintain knowledge of professional information related to the services they render.

a. Professional counselors accurately represent their competence, education, training and experience.

b. As teachers, professional counselors perform their duties based on careful preparation so that their instruction is accurate, up-to-date, and scholarly.

c. Professional counselors recognize the need for continuing training to prepare themselves to serve persons of all ages and cultural backgrounds. They are open to new procedures and sensitive to differences between groups of people and changes in expectations and values over time.

d. Professional counselors with the responsibility for decisions involving individuals or policies based on test results should have an understanding of counseling or educational measurement, validation problems and other test research. Test users should know and understand the literature relevant to the tests used and testing problems with which they deal.

e. Professional counselors/practitioners recognize that their effectiveness depends in part upon their ability to maintain sound interpersonal relations, that temporary or more enduring aberrations on their part may interfere with their abilities or distort their appraisals of others. Therefore, they refrain from undertaking any activity in which the personal problems are likely to lead to inadequate professional services or harm to a client; or, if they are already engaged in such activity when they become aware of their personal problems, they would seek competent professional assistance to determine whether they should suspend or terminate services to one or all of their clients.

PRINCIPLE 3. MORAL AND LEGAL STANDARDS

Professional counselors' moral, ethical and legal standards of behavior are a personal matter to the same degree as they are for any other citizen, except as these may compromise the fulfillment of their professional responsibilities, or reduce the trust in counseling or counselors held by the general public. Regarding their own behavior, professional counselors should be aware of the prevailing community standards and of the possible impact upon the quality of professional services provided by their conformance to or deviation from these standards. Professional counselors should also be aware of the possible impact of their public behavior upon the ability of colleagues to perform their professional duties.

a. To protect public confidence in the profession of counseling, professional counselors will avoid public behavior that is clearly in violation of accepted moral and legal standards.

b. To protect students, counselors/teachers will be aware of the diverse backgrounds of students and, when dealing with topics that may give offense, will see that the material is treated objectively, that it is clearly relevant to the course, and that it is treated in a manner for which the student is prepared.

c. Providers of counseling services conform to the statutes relating to such services as established by the Commonwealth of Virginia and the Virginia Board of Professional Counselors.

d. As employees, professional counselors refuse to participate in employer's practices which are inconsistent with the moral and legal standards established by federal or state legislation regarding the treatment of employees or of the public. In particular and for example, professional counselors will not condone practices which result in illegal or otherwise unjustifiable discrimination on the basis of race, sex, religion or national origin in hiring, promotion or training.

e. In providing counseling services to clients, professional counselors avoid any action that will violate or diminish the legal and civil rights of clients or of others who may be affected by the action.

PRINCIPLE 4. PUBLIC STATEMENTS

Professional counselors in their professional roles may be expected or required to make public statements providing counseling information, professional opinions, or supply information about the availability of counseling products and services. In making such statements, professional counselors take full account of the limits and uncertainties of present counseling knowledge and techniques. They represent, as objectively as possible, their professional qualifications, affiliations, and functions, as well as those of the institution or organization with which the statements may be associated. All public statements, announcements of services, and promotional activities should serve the purpose of providing sufficient information to aid the consumer public in making informed judgments and choices on matters that concern it.

a. When announcing professional services, professional counselors limit the information to: name, highest relevant degree conferred, certification or licensure, address, telephone number, office hours, cost of services, and a brief explanation of the types of services rendered. Such statements will be descriptive of services offered but not evaluative as to their quality of uniqueness. They will not contain testimonials by quotation or by implication. They will not claim uniqueness of skills or methods beyond those available to others in the profession unless determined by acceptable and public scientific evidence.

b. In announcing the availability of counseling services or products professional counselors will not display their affiliations with organizations or agencies in a manner that implies the sponsorship or certification of the organization or agency. They will not name their employer or professional associations unless the services are in fact to be provided by or under the responsible, direct supervision and continuing control of such organizations or agencies.

c. Professional counselors associated with the development or promotion of counseling devices, books, or other products offered for commercial sale will make every effort to insure that announcements and advertisements are represented in a professional and factually informative manner without unsupported claims of superiority over devices, books and products of similar purpose. Claims of superiority must be supported by scientifically acceptable evidence or by willingness to aid and encourage independent professional scrutiny or scientific test.

d. Professional counselors engaged in radio, television or other public media activities will not participate in commercial announcements recommending to the general public the purchase or use of any proprietary or single-source product or service.

e. Professional counselors who describe counseling or the services of professional counselors to the general public accept the obligation to present the material fairly and accurately, avoiding misrepresentation through sensationalism, exaggeration or superficiality. Professional counselors will be guided by the primary obligation to aid the public in forming their own informed judgments, opinions and choices.

f. As teachers, professional counselors ensure that statements in catalogs and course outlines are accurate, particularly in terms of subject matter to be covered, bases for grading, and nature of classroom experiences. As practitioners providing private services, professional counselors avoid improper, direct solicitation of clients and the conflict of interest inherent therein.

g. Professional counselors accept the obligation to correct others who may represent their professional qualifications or associations with products or services in a manner incompatible with these guidelines.

PRINCIPLE 5. CONFIDENTIALITY

Professional counselors have a primary obligation to safeguard information about individuals obtained in the course of teaching, practice or research. Personal information is communicated to others only with the person's written consent or in those circumstances where there is clear and imminent danger to the client, to others or to society. Disclosures of counseling information are restricted to what is necessary, relevant, and verifiable.

a. All materials in the official record shall be shared with the client who shall have the right to decide what information may be shared with anyone beyond the immediate provider of service and to be informed of the implications of the materials to be shared.

b. The anonymity of clients served in public and other agencies is preserved, if at all possible, by withholding names and personal identifying data. If external conditions require reporting such information, the client shall be so informed.

c. Information received in confidence by one agency or person shall not be forwarded to another person or agency without the client's written permission.

d. Service providers have a responsibility to insure the accuracy and to indicate the validity of data shared with their parties.

e. Case reports presented in classes, professional meetings, or in publications shall be so disguised that no identification is possible unless the client or responsible authority has read the report and agreed in writing to its presentation or publication.

f. Counseling reports and records are maintained under conditions of security and provisions are made for their destruction when they have outlived their usefulness. Professional counselors insure that privacy and confidentiality are maintained by all persons in the employ or volunteer services of the agency or office, including clerical staff, students, volunteers, and community aides.

g. Professional counselors who ask that an individual reveal personal information in the course of interviewing, testing, or evaluation, or who allow such information to be divulged, do so only after making certain that the person or authorized representative is fully aware of the purposes of the interview, testing or evaluation and of the ways in which the information will be used.

h. Sessions with clients are taped or otherwise recorded only with their written permission or the written permission of a responsible guardian. Even with guardian written consent one should not record a session against the expressed wishes of a client.

i. Where a child or adolescent is the primary client, the interests of the minor shall be paramount.

j. In work with families, the rights of each family member should be safeguarded. The provider of service also has the responsibility to discuss the contents of the record with the parent and/or child, as appropriate, and to keep separate those parts which should remain the property of each family member.

PRINCIPLE 6. WELFARE OF THE CONSUMER

Professional counselors respect the integrity and protect the welfare of the people and groups with whom they work. When there is a conflict of interest between the client and the professional counselors' employing institution, the professional counselors clarify the nature and direction of their loyalties and responsibilities and keep all parties informed of their commitments. Professional counselors fully inform consumers as to the purpose and nature of any evaluative, treatment, educational or training procedure, and they freely acknowledge that clients, students, or subjects have freedom of choice with regard to participation.

a. Professional counselors are continually cognizant both of their own needs and of their inherently powerful position "vis-a-vis" clients, in order to avoid exploiting the client's trust and dependency. Professional counselors make every effort to avoid dual relationships with clients and/or relationships which might impair their professional judgment or increase the risk of client exploitation. Examples of such dual relationships include treating an employee or supervisee, treating a close friend or family relative, and sexual relationships with clients.

b. Where professional counselors work with members of an organization goes beyond reasonable conditions of employment, professional counselors recognize possible conflicts of interests that may arise. When such conflicts occur, professional counselors clarify the nature of the conflict and inform all parties of the nature and directions of the loyalties and responsibilities involved.

c. When acting as supervisors, trainers, or employers, professional counselors accord recipients informed choice, confidentiality, and protection from physical and mental harm.

d. Financial arrangements in professional practice are in accord with professional standards that safeguard the best interests of the client and that are clearly understood by the client in advance of billing. This may best be done by the use of a contract. Professional counselors are responsible for assisting clients in finding needed services in those instances where payment of the usual fee would be a hardship. No commission or rebate or other form of remuneration may be given or received for referral of clients for professional services, whether by an individual or by an agency.

e. Professional counselors are responsible for making their services readily accessible to clients in a manner that facilitates the client's ability to make an informed choice when selecting a service provider. This responsibility includes a clear written description of what the client may expect in the way of tests, reports, billing, therapeutic regime and schedules.

f. Professional counselors who find that their services are not beneficial to the client have the responsibility to make this known to the responsible persons.

g. Professional counselors are accountable to the parties who refer and support counseling services and to the general public and are cognizant of the indirect or long-range effects of their intervention.

h. The professional counselor attempts to terminate a private service or consulting relationship when it is reasonably clear to the professional counselor that the consumer is not benefitting from it. If a consumer is receiving services from another mental health professional, professional counselors do not offer their services directly to the consumer without informing the professional persons already involved in order to avoid confusion and conflict for the consumer.

PRINCIPLE 7. PROFESSIONAL RELATIONSHIPS

Professional counselors act with due regard to the needs and feelings of their colleagues in counseling and other professions. Professional counselors respect the prerogatives and obligations of the institutions or organizations with which they are associated.

a. Professional counselors understand the areas of competence of related professions and make full use of other professional, technical, and administrative resources which best serve the interests of consumers. The absence of formal relationships with other professional workers does not relieve professional counselors from the responsibility of securing for their clients the best possible professional service; indeed, this circumstance presents a challenge to the professional competence of professional counselors, requiring special sensitivity to problems outside their areas of training, and foresight, diligence, and tact in obtaining the professional assistance needed by clients.

b. Professional clients know and take into account the traditions and practices of other professional groups with which they work and cooperate fully with members of such groups when research, services, and other functions are shared or in working for the benefit of public welfare.

c. Professional counselors strive to provide positive conditions for those they employ and that they spell out clearly the conditions of such employment. They encourage their employees to engage in activities that facilitate their further professional development.

d. Professional counselors respect the viability, reputation, and the proprietary right of organizations which they service. Professional counselors show due regard for the interests of their present or prospective employers. In those instances where they are critical of programs or policies, they attempt to effect change by constructive actions within the organization.

e. In the pursuit of research, professional counselors give sponsoring agencies, host institutions, and publication channels the same respect and opportunity for giving informed consent that they accord to individual research participants. They are aware of their obligation to future research workers and insure that host institutions are given feedback information and proper acknowledgement.

f. Credit is assigned to those who have contributed to a publication, in proportion to their contribution.

g. When a professional counselor violates ethical standards, professional counselors who know first-hand of such activities should, if possible, attempt to rectify the situation. Failing an informal solution, professional counselors should bring such unethical activities to the attention of the Virginia Board of Professional Counselors.

PRINCIPLE 8. UTILIZATION OF ASSESSMENT TECHNIQUES

In the development, publication, and utilization of counseling assessment techniques, professional counselors folllow relevant standards. Individuals examined, or their legal guardians, have the right to know the results, the interpretation made, and where appropriate, the particulars on which final judgment was based. Test users should take precautions to protect test security but not at the expense of an individual's right to understand the basis for decisions that adversely affect that individual or that individual's dependents.

a. The client has the right to have and the provider has the responsibility to give explanations of test results in language the client can understand.

b. When a test is published or otherwise made available for operational use, it should be accompanied by a manual (or other published or readily available information) that makes every reasonable effort to describe fully the development of the test, the rationale, specifications followed in writing items or selecting observations, and procedures and results of item analysis or other research. The test, the manual, the record forms and other accompanying material should help users make correct interpretations of the test results, and should warn against common misuses. The test manual should state explicitly the purposes and applications for which the test is recommended and identify any special qualifications required to administer the test and to interpret it properly. Evidence of validity and reliability, along with other relevant research data, should be presented in support of any claims made.

c. Norms presented in test manuals should refer to defined and clearly described populations. These populations should be the groups with whom users of the test will ordinarily wish to compare the persons tested. Test users should consider the possibility of bias in tests or in test items. When indicated, there should be an investigation of possible differences in validity for ethnic, sex, or other subsamples that can be identified when the test is given.

d. Professional counselors who have the responsibility for decisions about individuals or policies that are based on test results should have a thorough understanding of counseling or educational measurement and of validation and other test research.

e. Professional counselors should develop procedures for systematically eliminating from data files test score information that has, because of the lapse of time, become obsolete.

f. Any individual or organization offering test scoring and interpretation services must be able to demonstrate that their programs are based on appropriate research to establish the validity of the programs and procedures used in arriving at interpretations. The public offering of an automated test interpretation service will be considered as a professional-to-professional consultation. In this the formal responsibility of the consultant is to the consultee but his/her ultimate and overriding responsibility is to the client.

g. Counseling services for the purpose of diagnosis, treatment, or personalized advice are provided only in the context of a professional relationship, and are not given by means of public lectures or demonstrations, newspaper or magazine articles, radio or television programs, mail, or similar media. The preparation of personnel reports and recommendations based on test data secured solely by mail is unethical unless such appraisals are an integral part of a continuing client relationship with a company, as a result of which the consulting professional counselor has intimate knowledge of the client's personal situations and can be assured thereby that his written appraisals will be adequate to the purpose and will be properly interpreted by the client. These reports must not be embellished with such detailed analyses of the subject's personality traits as would be appropriate only after intensive interviews with the subject.

PRINCIPLE 9. PURSUIT OF RESEARCH ACTIVITIES

The decision to undertake research should rest upon a considered judgment by the individual professional counselor about how best to contribute to counseling and to human welfare. Professional counselors carry out their investigations with respect for the people who participate and with concern for their dignity and welfare.

a. In planning a study the investigator has the personal responsibility to make a careful evaluation of its ethical acceptability, taking into account the following principles for research with human beings. To the extent that this appraisal, weighting scientific and humane values, suggests a deviation from any principle, the investigator incurs an increasingly serious obligation to seek ethical advice and to observe more stringent safeguards to protect the rights of the human research participants.

b. Professional counselors know and take into account the traditions and practices of other professional groups with which they work and cooperate fully with members of such groups when research, services, and other functions are shared or in working for the benefit of public welfare.

c. Ethical practice requires the investigator to inform the participant of all features of the research that reasonably might be expected to influence willingness to participate, and to explain all other aspects of the research about which the participant inquires. Failure to make full disclosure gives added emphasis to the investigators abiding responsibility to protect the welfare and dignity of the research participant.

d. Openness and honesty are essential characteristics of the relationship between investigator and research participant. When the methodological requirements of a study necessitate concealment or deception, the investigator is required to insure as soon as possible the participant's understanding of the reasons for this action and to restore the quality of the relationship with the investigator.

e. In the pursuit of research, professional counselors give sponsoring agencies, host institutions, and publications channels the same respect and opportunity for giving informed consent that they accord to individual research participants. They are aware of their obligation to future research workers and insure that host institutions are given feedback information and proper acknowledgement.

f. Credit is assigned to those who have contributed to a publication, in proportion to their contribution.

g. The ethical investigator protects participants from physical and mental discomfort, harm and danger. If the risk of such consequences exists, the investigator is required to inform the participant of that fact, secure consent before proceeding, and take all possible measures to minimize distress. A research procedure may not be used if it is likely to cause serious and lasting harm to participants.

h. After the data are collected, ethical practice requires the investigator to provide the participant with a full clarification of the nature of the study and to remove any misconceptions that may have arisen. Where scientific or humane values justify delaying or withholding information, the investigator acquires a special responsibility to assure that there are no damaging consequences for the participants.

i. Where research procedures may result in undesirable consequences for the participant, the investigator has the responsibility to detect and remove or correct these consequences, including, where relevant, long-term aftereffects.

j. Information obtained about the research participants during the course of an investigation is confidential. When the possibility exists that others may obtain access to such information, ethical research practice requires that the possibility, together with the plans for protecting confidentiality, be explained to the participants as a part of the procedure for obtaining informed consent.

NEED TO BE INFORMED

Callis (1979) declared that there is a considerable body of law that directly impinges on the practice of counseling. "It is equally abundantly clear that counselor and counselor educators are not conversant with this body of law. A perusal of professional journals [APGA and APA journals] reveal almost no articles dealing with this body of law. An examination of representative college catalogs reveal very few courses available to counselors on this topic" (Callis, 1979, 206). Van Hoose in 1980 states that

> any profession so widely practiced and having such potential for both positive and negative influences must pay particular attention to the ethical principles and issues that find their way into professional practice. Clearly, ethics has received far too little attention in the counseling profession. For example, many students in counseling are obtaining graduate degrees without ever having had more than a lecture or two on professional ethics. And many people now working as fulltime counselors have little understanding of the ethical implications of their work. These are serious omissions that must be dealt with if counseling is to receive the public acceptance and legal recognition necessary for true professional status. I view this matter as critical to the future of the profession. (P. 1)

Within the last decade, laws and regulations concerning counseling have increased. During this time consumers have come to expect more and better services; likewise, they have become aware of their legal rights. Consequently, more than at any other time in the history of counseling, counselors must know their legal boundaries and responsibilities.

There are several clues strongly suggesting that counselors may face more litigation in the future. For example, the American Association for Counseling and Development (formerly APGA) and the American Psychological Association encourage members to carry liability insurance. Also, counselors function in a variety of work settings that introduce a range of problems that can lead to potential liability charges. Today's counselors are assertive and open to new techniques and approaches. This atitude too opens the door for litigation.

For specific legal problems, counselors should consult attorneys. However, there are several ways in which counselors may be better prepared and may prevent legal problems.

1. Counselors should become familiar with federal and state laws concerning their profession.
2. Counselors should be familiar with state school department and local school regulations related to their work.

3. Counselors should become familiar with court decisions related to counseling.
4. Counselors should be familiar with and follow the ethical standards and guidelines offered by their professional organizations.

The need of practitioners in the helping professions for legal information is obvious, not only for their own protection and to guard the integrity of the profession and confidence of the consumer but to protect the health, welfare, and rights of the consumer as well.

CHAPTER GUIDELINES

1. Counseling is an important emerging profession that has become a major social force and is becoming a profound influence on individuals and public beliefs and public policy.
2. Counselor role and control, professional maturity, and primary/secondary commitments of the professional practitioner are enmeshed with legal and ethical concerns.
3. Ethical standards adopted by professional counseling groups and by state licensing regulations are becoming the benchmarks by which all who are in the helping professions are assessed.

SITUATIONAL DISCUSSIONS

Situation 1: As a counselor in an agency, school, mental health center, or in private practice, identify your primary and secondary commitments, and review the codes of ethics, statutes, and regulations that affect your role and control.

Situation 2: Determine the extent to which public (state and local) employment as a counselor contrasts or compares with private practice.

Situation 3: Identify those aspects of your professional code of ethics that also carry legal implications for your practice as a counselor.

Situation 4: Review your personal practice as a professional counselor in light of the ten most frequent legal and ethical questions that arise.

Situation 5: Check the four items listed on pages 21-22 and determine the extent to which you are familiar with each of the sources listed.

REFERENCES

Allport, G., 1961, *Pattern and Growth in Personality,* Holt, Rinehart and Winston, New York.

Beers, C., 1956, *A Mind That Found Itself,* 5th ed., Doubleday, Garden City, N.Y.

Belkin, G., 1975, *Practical Counseling in the Schools,* William C. Brown, Dubuque, Iowa.

Bui, J., 1983 (August), North Carolina enacts registration law, *Guidepost,* **25,** pp. 1-7.

Callis, R., 1979, Counseling and guidance and the law, in *The Status of Guidance and Counseling in the Nation's Schools,* American Personnel and Guidance Association, Washington, D.C., pp. 191-210.

Dunlop, R., 1968, *Professional Problems in School Counseling Practice,* International Textbook, Scranton, Pa.

Ellis, A., 1962, *Reason and Emotion in Psychotherapy,* Lyle Stuart, New York.

Ethical principles of psychologists, 1981, *American Psychologist* **36:**633-638.

Ethical Standards of the American Personnel and Guidance Association, 1981, Washington, D.C.

Fretz, B., and D. Mills, 1980, *Licensing and Certification of Psychologists and Counselors,* Jossey-Bass, Washington, D.C.

Hummel, D., 1980, The counselor: Ethical standards and the law, *Virginia Personnel and Guidance Journal* **8**(1):26-30.

Hummel, D., and C. Humes, 1984, *Pupil Services: Development, Coordination and Administration,* Macmillan, Boston.

Lloyd-Jones, E., and E. Westervelt, eds., 1963, *Behavioral Science and Guidance,* Columbia University, New York.

McCully, C., 1963, Professionalization: Symbol or substance? *Counselor Education and Supervision* **2:**106-112.

Mathewson, R., 1963, The meaning of maturity in guidance: An inquiry, in *The Meaning of Maturity,* Pupil Services Series, Ohio University Center for Educational Research and Service, Athens, Ohio, pp. 1-12.

Menninger, W., 1954 (September 11), Menninger lists 8 points for maturity, *New York Herald Tribune,* p. 24.

Mora, G., 1975, History and theoretical trends in psychiatry, in *Psychiatry/II,* 2nd ed., vol. 1, A. Freedman, H. Kaplan, and B. Sadoctz, eds., Williams & Wilkins, Baltimore, pp. 1-75.

Northrup, F., 1946, *The Meeting of East and West,* Macmillan, New York.

Nugent, F., 1981, *Professional Counseling: An Overview,* Brooks/Cole, Monterey, Calif.

Parsons, F., 1967, *Choosing a Vocation,* Agathon Press, New York.

Rogers, C., 1974, In retrospect—Forty-six years, *American Psychologist* **19**(2):115-123.

Smith, T., and W. Debbins, 1945, *Constructive Ethics,* Prentice-Hall, New York.

Tolbert E., 1978, *An Introduction to Guidance,* Little, Brown, Boston.

Talbutt, L., and D. Hummel, 1982, Legal issues impacting on counselors, *Counseling and Human Development* **14**(2):1-12.

Van Hoose, W., 1980, Ethics and counseling, *Counseling and Human Development* **13**(1):1-12.

Van Hoose, W., and J. Kottler, 1977, *Ethical and Legal Issues in Counseling and Psychotherapy,* Jossey-Bass, San Francisco.

Virginia State Board of Professional Counselors, 1977, Section J, ethical standards, in *Regulations,* Department of Professional and Occupational Regulations, Richmond, Va.

Chapter 2

Ethical Standards

Almost all recognized professions have adopted a code and system of ethics. Such codes and systems make up the ethical standards that provide guidelines for professional practice and behavior. The counseling profession is among those that have adopted ethical standards for its members. Besides ethical standards, a considerable body of law directly impinges on the practice of counseling and guidance. However, the hallmark of a profession is that its members adopt standards of practice and adhere to such standards in providing their services. Ethical standards stipulate conditions for professional behavior for the practitioner. Ethical standards also define services to be provided that are appropriate to training and competencies of practioners in the profession. It is assumed that laws of credentialing and licensing will provide the bases for entry into practice. As Flexner (1910) found in his 1910 Carnegie Foundation study of medical school education, there exists today a wide diversity of standards, curricula, and organization in the education for the helping professions. Because of this wide diversity, codes of ethics tend to become the bases for judging practice, consumer protection, and legal considerations.

THREE ETHICAL CODES

For counselors, three basic statements of ethical practice and behavior apply to work in the profession. Two of these statements are the *Ethical*

Standards (1981) of the American Personnel and Guidance Association (APGA) and the "Ethical Principles of Psychologists" (1981) of the American Psychological Association (APA). Members of the associations are expected to practice these codes of ethics and professional standards. Failure to abide by the standards may result in being expelled from membership in the association. A third statement of ethical standards is contained in regulations pertaining to counselor licensure. Among such standards the Virginia regulations will be cited as an example of a legal regulation for counselors. A statement of ethical standards is contained within the *Regulations* of the Virginia State Board of Professional Counselors (1977) as section 5, "Ethical Standards." These standards can, in effect, be viewed as law as well as a code of ethics. A breach of the stated code of ethics can result in litigation against a professional counselor and possible revocation of license.

Ethical standards adopted by the two professional associations cited previously and by the Virginia Board of Professional Counselors tend to cover many of the same aspects of practice, although topics within the codes vary. Table 2-1, which compares the topics of these three codes, covers the scope of counselor practice for practitioners (Talbutt and Hummel, 1982). According to an unofficial opinion of a judge, the several codes of ethics mentioned here would apply to counselor practice whether or not the counselor holds professional association membership or is a licensed professional counselor.

Basically, these standards are concerned with counselor responsibilities, competence, client relationships, and confidentiality. In addition, both APA and several divisions of APGA have adopted the following standards for measurement and evaluation: *Standards for Educational and Psychological Tests and Manuals* (1973) and "Responsibilities of Users" (1978). Specific applications of the APGA ethical standards appropriate to each of the topical statements are illustrated in the *Ethical Standards Casebook by Callis (1976).*

ETHICAL STANDARDS AS A GUIDE TO PRACTICE

Recently, "Lemons from a Shady Dealer" (Leo, 1983) appeared as the title of an article in which the value of all therapy was questioned. In *The Shrinking of America,* Zilbergeld (1983) arives at a conclusion close to Hans Eysenck's that clients of counselors and psychotherapists usually feel better and treatment results in some positive changes in their lives, but such changes are modest and short-lived. Although Zilbergeld and Eysenck's conclusions dealt with the results of research in psychotherapy (the treatment of persons considered neurotic or psychotic), their research nevertheless reflects on the work of all counselors. What are the goals of counselors and

Table 2-1. Ethical Standards Topics

American Personnel and Guidance Association	*American Psychological Association*	*Virginia Board of Professional Counselors*
A. General (member responsibility, professional services, and interprofessional relationships)	1. Responsibility	1. Responsibility
B. Counseling Relationship	2. Competence	2. Competence
C. Measurement and Evaluation	3. Moral and Legal Standards	3. Moral and Legal Standards
D. Research	4. Misrepresentation	4. Public Statements
E. Consulting	5. Confidentiality	5. Confidentiality
F. Private Practice	6. Welfare of the Consumer	6. Welfare of the Consumer
G. Personnel Administration	7. Professional Relationships	7. Professional Relationships
H. Preparation Standards	8. Assessment Techniques	8. Utilization of Assessment
	9. Research with Human Participants	9. Pursuit of Research Activities
	10. Care and Use of Animals	

what values underlie these goals? The question is one that if left unanswered could challenge the survival of counselors and their work. A quality performance with positive results must be ethically based and consistent with the values of the democratic ideal.

Goals, according to this ideal, are to guard the rights of the individuals, to ensure development, and to enlarge opportunity—the root faith clients bring to counselors. Major emphasis and responsibility supporting the concept of a free society rest on a system of universal services. Counseling philosophy must encompass an appreciation of the worth and dignity of the individual, realization of individual differences among humans, and a recognition of humanity's inherent rights of self-direction and choice. Over the years counseling helped maintain our beliefs in these concepts in the face of many challenges, and it helped us to progress in providing basic learing experiences resulting in scientific and social accomplishments unequalled among nations of the world. We have been considerably less successful in direct assistance to individuals (through counseling and teaching) when conflict of values are in question.

Generally recognized to be in accord with goals of counseling is the realization that effective counseling through social interaction is the core of the process. It is also recognized that this task is largely dependent upon accurate knowledge of the client's personal characteristics, which include potential, interests, and ambitions. Recognition of these individual factors, along with the adaptation of methods and the provision of a healthy environment for learning, provides for the motivational factors for individual development and change. Furthermore, it is recognized that realistic self-direction by the client relies on a continuous understanding of self in relation to potential, oportunities, obligations, and responsibility in our society. However, faith and the freedom to act in a society may suffer from a lack of understanding and demands of individual responsibility for action. Conflict may surface.

THE CONFLICT BETWEEN GOALS AND PERFORMANCE

With regard to the counseling setting, an obvious and prominent type of predicament is the conflict between the expectations of the specific social institution and the values of the general society; for example, it is generally expected by the school that the students will work diligently to achieve to the fullest extent of their intellectual potentiality and creativity. Accordingly, they must be motivated to sacrifice immediate ease for ultimate attainment. However, recent commentaries suggest that our social values tend to prize ease and sociability more than intellectual independence and achievement. Several of the conflicts between values and performances are obvious from what we say we value and how we act in the counseling process.

We value the individual's potential and her or his right to make personal decisions. But we often show an unexpressed bias and a discomfort that prompts us to feel that a decision will be more valid if it matches the one we have selected.

We value the notion that there is no single niche into which an individual fits. We believe that for each individual there are alternative choices. But we tend to overemphasize so-called objective data in selecting the best pigeonhole for the individual.

We value the dignity of all work. But we also believe that each should fulfill her or his highest potential, so we urge the bright to enter status professions and overlook others, especially in the realm of social and governmental services.

We value the teaching and learning in counseling process as a focusing on the total development of the individual. But we allow this process to be influenced by whatever pressures our time and culture force on us.

We value communication as a basic aspect of social interaction through counseling. But we assume that the spoken work has usually the same meaning for counselor and client.

We value the premise that every individual is a unique personality. But we have a sterotype of the ideal, and we typify some by their background and by our own.

We value the proposition that clients bring to the counselor's office the sum of their experiences. But we often act as if counseling were an isolated process unrelated to the world of which they are a part.

We value the ideal that all persons deserve the acceptance, understanding, and assistance of a professional counselor. But we often relegate such efforts to problem situations with no time for the rest. The temptation may be to refer the individual to the social agency rather than assist him/her as we do counselees with other concerns.

We value the importance of a significant model for growing individuals. But as the senior generation, we often tend to isolate ourselves from true helping relationships through social interaction in which a model can be perceived by younger clients.

We value the significance of the relationship that can be developed behind the closed doors of the counselor's office. Yet this may not be where the action is with our clients. The real action may be political, economic, or social in the form of protest, dissent, usually in the name of individual freedom or social justice.

ETHICS, JUDGMENT, AND MORAL VALUES

Law, whether enacted by a legislature or established by case law, is established to decide and insure legal and moral justice. However, laws cannot precisely decide what a member of a helping profession should do. Neither in many cases can ethical standards avoid degrees of subjective judgment. Even though standards are stipulated, each practitioner tends to have a unique style of ethics. "Most styles (however) have common elements, in that the mode is consistent with societal standards and expectations as well as . . . the criteria of professional, social, religious, and ethnic groups" (Van Hoose and Kottler, 1977, 19). What this means for counseling practitioners is that ethics based on personal moral values guides an individual's judgment.

In the counseling process, decisions made and actions taken are frequently mutually agreed upon by client and counselor, which fuses moral values of both. Such a process is consistent with the concept of recipriocity—an interpersonal and mutual state of trust and respect for each other's concept of morality. However, it is the counselor who, in the process, weighs the ethical judgment factor. How then is moral commitment and development to be judged by the counselor? As a guide in responding to the vital question, Hoffman (1970, 277-278) classifies moral and ethical behavior into the following four factors, which are seen as aspects of most counseling cases:

1. *Internalized moral code.* The counselors have the ability to resist temptation. They will not engage in unethical practices even if they know they cannot be detected. They are motivated to please themselves rather than others.
2. *Sense of guilt.* They feel badly when they do something wrong. They have an internalized conscience that works to remind them of ethically sound behavior.
3. *Personal standards.* They have the capacity to rely on their personal beliefs and moral standards rather than on one externally imposed.
4. *Responsibility for actions.* They accept responsibility for the consequences of their behavior.

ASSETS AND LIMITATIONS

According to Talbutt, ethical standards are both assets and limitations to the counseling profession.* Ethical standards are generally adopted to help clarify a professional's responsibilities to consumer clients, to employing agencies, and to society at large. Such standards become referral sources for the courts, and here conflicts and litigation matters come into play. Interpretations of standards and application to evidence are often a matter for the courts to decide. Frequently the situation, the setting, or the conflict will affect such interpretations.

Ethical Standards (1981) does not address the behavior of counselors in every situation. Instead, it comprises broad principles "which must be interpreted and applied . . . to a particular context" (Strude and McKelvey, 1979, 453). Daubner and Daubner (1970, 433) defined ethics as the "principles or norms that ought to govern human conduct." According to Van Hoose

---

*This section is revised and adapted from L. Talbutt, 1981, Ethical standards: Assets and limitations, *Personnel and Guidance Journal* **60:**110-112, with permission.

and Kottler (1977), ethical standards help counselors deal with three groups: clients, professionals, and the public. Van Hoose and Kottler (1978, 8) also posit three reasons why professional codes of ethics exist:

> First, ethical standards are designed to protect the profession from the government. All professions desire autonomy and seek to avoid interference and regulations by lawmakers. They prefer to regulate themselves through professional codes or standards rather than risk regulations from legislative bodies.
>
> Second, ethical standards protect the professions from the self-destruction of internal bickering.
>
> Finally ethical standards are designed to protect the therapist from the public. If he behaves within the code he has some protection for malpractice.

In summary, ethical standards are significant in three ways: they are self imposed regulations, they prevent internal disagreement, and they provide protection in case of litigation. The first two statements need little explanation, but the last one should be considered at some length owing to recent litigation (Talbutt and Hummel, 1982).

Ethics and Civil Liability

Standards of ethics stand as both an asset and a potential liability for a practictioner. Although ethical codes present guidelines for practice, they do not provide the crucial questions regarding a counselor's behavior. Behavior, from a legal standpoint, requires description and labeling of actions taken in the counseling process. Criteria for identifying, describing, and labeling counselor behavior where liability comes into question are presented by Vriend and Dyer (1976) as follows:

> 1. Is the behavior in question self-defeating?
> 2. Where and when does the behavior occur?
> 3. How often and to what degree is the behavior manifested?
> 4. What are the circumstances under which the behavior occurs?
> 5. Are there any evident patterns to which the behavior seems connected? (P. 84)

When reviewing the evidence produced by responding to the above questions, both law and ethics come into play, and at times the contradictory evidence can result in a civil liability allegation. Specifically, the issues involved in assessment, referral, consultation, counselor-client relationship, discrimination, and client behavior as a result of counseling can be evaluated for possible liability.

Counselors, social workers, and a variety of educators and other professionals face potential civil liability litigation. (See chapters 6 and 7.) Therefore, professionals should come to understand some major areas that could lead to civil liability litigation. Civil liability means that a person can be sued "for not doing right or for doing wrong to another" (Burgum and Anderson, 1975, 25). Professionals are expected to follow certain legal standards of conduct to their work, and when they do not, court action can result. The two types of civil liabilities are constitutional and common torts. The discussion in this chapter is limited to liabilities related to common torts. Alexander, Corns, and McCann (1969, 324) described *tort* as "any civil wrong independent of contract" and summarized:

> The law grants to each individual certain personal rights not of a contractual nature, such as freedom from personal injury and security of life, liberty, and property. The law imposes corresponding duties and responsibilities on each individual to respect these rights of others. If, by speech or other conduct, we fail to respect these rights, thereby damaging another individual, we have committed a tort and may be financially liable for our action. (P. 324)

Ethical standards may offer protection for counselors against litigation. Because counselors are judged by standards suitable to their profession, Burgum and Anderson concluded that if—as in the field of medicine—they act in good faith, they are probably not responsible for a client's lack of progress or a mistake in judgment if the mistake were the type a "careful and skillful" counselor could make (Burgum and Anderson, 1975, 34).

Counselors, like physicians, are expected to display behavior suitable to their profession. "The law imposes on a physician who undertakes the care of a patient the obligation of due care, the exercise of an amount of skill common to his profession, without which he should not have taken the case, and a degree of care commensurate with this position" (61 Am. Jur. 2d 201).

Also, physicians have a duty to act in good faith and advise patients regarding the best possible treatment.

> The main obligation of the physician imposed upon him by law is the exercise of due care and skill in the treatment of his patient. The physician's duty of due care includes among others, his obligation to fully inform the patient of his condition, to continue to provide for medical care once the patient-physician relationship has been established, to refer him to a specialist if necessary, and to obtain the patient's informed consent to the medical treatment or operation. (61 Am. Jur. 2d 167)

Similarly, counselors are expected to refer clients to another professional when necessary. "If the member determines an inability to be of professional assistance to the client, the member must either avoid initiating the counseling relationship or immediately terminate the relationship. In either event, the member must suggest appropriate alternatives" (*Ethical Standards,* 1981, section B-10).

Counselors are expected to behave according to the standards of their profession. Appropriate guidelines for such behavior exist in *Ethical Standards.* Counselors, like physicians, are also expected to act in good faith and refer clients when appropriate. This expectation is also spelled out in *Ethical Standards.* In case of litigation, a counselor's conduct would probably be judged in terms of behavior appropriate to other professionals with similar qualifications and duties. The ethical standards would likely be the basis for comparison.

Limitations

There are two major limitations of APGA's *Ethical Standards.* On one hand, there are conflicts within the standards. On the other, there are legal and ethical issues not covered by the standards. Thus, the ethical standards code must be supplemented by other information.

Alexander (1976) identified section A, "General," and section B, "Counseling Relationship," as two areas that present possible legal and ethical conflicts in the 1974 *Ethical Standards.* The same conflicts also exist in the 1981 *Ethical Standards,* portions of the two sections from which are identified below.

Section A. General

2. The member has a responsibility both to the individual who is served and to the institution within which the service is performed. . . . The acceptance of employment in an institution implies the member is in agreement with the general policies and principles of the institution. Therefore, the professional activities of the member are also in accord with the objectives of the institution.

Section B. Counseling Relationship

1. The member's *primary* obligation is to respect the integrity and promote the welfare of the client(s), whether the client(s) is (are) assisted individually or in a group relationship. . . .

4. When the client's condition indicates . . . danger to the client or others, the member must take reasonable personal action.

5. Records of the counseling relationship . . . are to be considered professional information . . . and they should not be considered a part of the records of the institution or agency in which the counselor is employed.

According to *Ethical Standards* cited above, "the member has responsibility both to the individual who is served and to the institution within which the service is performed" (p. 2). Alexander (1976) explained that public school counselors are not only responsible to their clients and institutions of employment but also to other students within the school. He established that the legal origin for this last area of responsibility falls within the police power of the state. The police power of the state was described as "the authority for requiring children to attend school under compulsory attendance statues" (Alexander, 1976, 226). Even though *Ethical Standards* (sec. B-1) indicates that the counselor's major concern should be the client, Alexander (1976, 227) wrote that there are times when the counselor as an "arm of the administration" must put the welfare of other students over that of the counselee. Thus he believed that school counselors should advise their clients of their limited relationship. Alexander maintained that the school counselor is in a "precarious ethical-legal position that must be balanced to insure the counselors of their rights and to insure the rights of others" (1976, 227).

One significant issue still unclear in *Ethical Standards* is section B,1 and 4. This section however, is even more confusing in terms of the court decision in *Tarasoff v. Regents of The University of California* (1974). In this case, Poddar—a patient of a psychotherapist employed at the University of California at Berkeley—told the psychotherapist that he intended to kill a particular person. The psychotherapist informed the university police, who detained Poddar for a short time and released him. Poddar then killed Tatiana Tarasoff. The parents sued the university regents, the psychotherapist, and campus police. The lower court found for the defendents, but on appeal the Supreme Court of California *(Tarasoff v. Regents of the University of California)* found the defendents negligent in their "duty to warn" (p. 565). The court concluded:

> We conclude that a doctor or a psychotherapist treating a mentally ill patient just as a doctor treating physical illness, bears a duty to use reasonable care to give threatened persons such warnings as are essential to avert forseeable danger arising from his patient's condition or treatment. (P. 559)

Ethical Standards (1981, sec. B-4) states a similar responsibility for counselors: "When the client's condition indicates . . . clear and imminent danger to the client or others, the member must take reasonable personal action or inform responsible authorities." On the surface the court decision in Tarasoff appears consistent with *Ethical Standards,* which spells out the counselor's duty to take action when there "is clear and imminent danger to the client or others."

In *Tarasoff* the psychotherapist warned the campus police who detained Poddar a short time and released him. However, the court determined that the person in danger should have been warned. Thus, notifying the campus police was not sufficient "warning," according to the court. In situations similar to *Tarasoff,* counselors must make professional judgments. Van Hoose and Kottler (1978) called for professional guidelines to help counselors make decisions in such situations. It is, indeed, crucial that counselors have some directions. For example, do school counselors warn minors, their parents, officials, or all three? There are no guidelines to aid counselors in this complex and confusing topic.

The 1981 APGA *Ethical Standards* provide general guidelines for professional behavior; however, the standards do not, nor should they, include specific court decisions and federal legislation. These materials must be obtained elsewhere. To deal with changing legal trends, APGA members should read professional journals devoted to recent court rulings and laws affecting counseling. Also, the APGA *Ethical Standards* addresses a national audience. Thus, state laws are not reflected. Counselors must obtain information on state laws from local and state professional groups and state journals.

Conflicts and unresolved issues in *Ethical Standards* indicate that there are times when counselors must seek additional information. The following conclusions should help counselors focus on the assets and limitations of *Ethical Standards.*

CHAPTER GUIDELINES

1. The major professional counseling associations have developed and adopted ethical codes, which mainly deal with counselor responsibilities, competence, client relationships, and confidentiality.
2. Counselors are human and thus must be aware of potential conflicts between goals and performance.
3. Ethical standards are both assets and limitations as they are related to legal conduct.
4. Civil liability, which is alleged with more frequency than in the past, requires members of the helping profession to be conversant with the law.
5. Even as the law is at times contradictory, especially case law, so are certain aspects of codes of ethics.

SITUATIONAL DISCUSSIONS

The following seven examples are cited after the *Ethical Standards Casebook* (Callis, 1976) as direct applications of selected sections of the APGA'S 1974 *Ethical Standards.*

Situation 1: An admissions officer in a college believes that some of the testing information transmission practices among the student personnel services are not ethical. He seeks consultation about these practices with his director. The director explains the background and rationale for the existing practices. The admissions officer concludes that the practices are consistent with his ethics and his institutional responsibility since he now knows that all faculty advisors receive intensive training about the test information they will be using (p. 13).

Application of Section A-2: The member has a responsibility both to the individual who is served and to the institution within which the service is performed (p. 13).

Situation 2: A counselor is facilitating a growth group session. At one point, one of the group expresses some personal concerns that indicate that he may have serious emotional problems. The counselor detects this and guides the group attention away from that group member. After the group meeting, the counselor privately encourages the person to seek individual counseling (p. 22).

Application of Section B-1: The member's primary obligation is to respect the integrity and promote the welfare of the counselee(s), whether the counselee(s) is(are) assisted individually or in a group relationship (p. 22).

Situation 3: A counselor in an elementary school interprets standardized tests to parents in three-way conferences including parents, teacher, and counselor. He finds that he can give a better evaluation of a student when the test results are related to classroom and home experiences. This provides the opportunity to discuss any necessary remedial steps that require cooperative action between the school and the home (p. 42).

Application of Section C-1: It is the member's responsibility to provide adequate orientation or information to the examinee(s) prior to and following the test administration so that the results of testing may be placed in proper perspective with other relevant factors. In so doing, the member must recognize the effects of socioeconomic, ethnic, and cultural factors on test scores (p. 42).

Situation 4: An investigator's research procedure calls for a rather long period of time from each subject. For some subjects the period would be extremely fatiguing and frustrating. He arranges the procedure so that there is a brief rest period at the end of each hour if the subject desires one. He also arranges for ample time to confer with all subjects as they finish to offer support, answer questions and the like (p. 54).

Application of Section D-1: In research with human subjects, researchers are responsible for their subjects' welfare throughout the experiment, and they must take all reasonable precautions to avoid causing injurious psychological, physical, or social effects on their subjects (p. 54).

Situation 5: A group of counseling consultants meet every other week in a group-discussion setting for the purpose of professional discussions. The sessions take on a group-counseling orientation, and it becomes obvious to the others that Consultant A has personal needs that would cause considerable trouble to any consultant-client relationship. Through the help of the group, Consultant A gains enough self-awareness to limit the cases with which he works to those problems that do not interefere with his personal limitations (p. 65).

Application of Section E-1: Members who act as a consultant must have a high degree of self-awareness of their own values and needs in entering helping relationships that involve change in social units (p. 65).

Situation 6: A large school decides to install a computer-assisted career information service under the supervision of the director of guidance. The director has no knowledge or skills regarding computers, so he recommends that he spend most of the summer taking computing courses at the university and visiting schools with computer-assisted career information services already in operation (p. 73).

Application of F-1: Members should define and describe the parameters and levels of their professional competency (p. 73).

Situation 7: A professor arranges practicum work for graduate students so that each student has at least one semester of supervised counseling in which the supervision is sufficiently intensive to provide one hour of supervision for each hour of practicum interviewing (p. 81).

Application of Section G-1: Members in charge of training are expected to establish programs that integrate academic study and supervised practice (p. 81).

REFERENCES

Alexander, D., 1976, Legal issues in guidance, in *School Guidance Services,* T. H. Hohenshil and J. H. Miles, eds., Kendall/Hunt, Dubuque, Iowa, pp. 233-259.

Alexander, K., R. Corns, and W. McCann, 1969, *Public School Law,* West Publ., St. Paul, Minn.

Burgum, T., and S. Anderson, 1975, *The Counselor and the Law,* American Personnel and Guidance Association, Washington, D.C.

Callis, R., ed., *Ethical Standards Casebook,* 2nd ed., American Personnel and Guidance Association, Washington, D.C.

Daubner, E. V., and E. S. Daubner, 1970, Ethics and counseling decisions, *Personnel and Guidance Journal,* **48:**433-436.

Ethical principles of psychologists, 1981, *American Psychologist* **36:**633-638.

Ethical Standards of the American Personnel and Guidance Association, 1981, Washington, D.C.

Flexner, A., 1910, *Medical Education in the United States and Canada,* Carnegie Foundation, New York.

Hoffman, M., 1970, Moral development, in *Carmichael's Manual of Child Psychology,* P. H. Mussen, ed., Wiley, New York, pp. 34-49.
Leo, J., 1983 (May 2), Lemons from a shady dealer, *Time,* p. 60.
Responsibilities of users of standardized tests, 1978, (October 1), *Guidpost,* pp. 5-8.
Standards for Educational and Psychological Tests and Manuals, 1973, American Psychological Association, Washington, D.C.
Strude, E. W., and J. McKelvey, 1979, Ethics and the law: Friend or foe? *Personnel and Guidance Journal* (May):453-456.
Talbutt, L. C., 1979, Law and Virginia Public School Counselors, unpublished doctoral dissertation, Virginia Polytechnic Institute and State University.
Talbutt, L. C., 1980, The counselor and state liability, *Virginia Personnel and Guidance Journal* **8:**37-41.
Talbutt, L. C., 1981, The medical rights of minors: Some answered and unanswered questions, *School Counselor* **27:**5.
Talbutt, L. C., 1981, Ethical standards: Assets and limitations, Personnel and Guidance Journal **60**(4):110-112.
Talbutt, L. C., and D. L. Hummel, 1982, Legal and ethical issues impacting on counselors, *Counseling and Human Development* **14**(2):1-12.
Van Hoose, W. H., and J. Kottler, 1977, *Ethical and Legal Issues in Counseling and Psychotherapy,* Jossey-Bass, San Francisco.
Virginia State Board of Professional Counselors, 1977, Section 5: Ethical standards, in *Regulations,* Department of Professional and Occupational Regulations, Richmond, Va.
Vriend, J., and W. Dyer, 1976, Creatively labeling behavior in individual and group counseling, *Journal of Marriage and Family Counseling* **2**(1):31-36.
Zilbergeld, B., 1982, *The Shrinking of America,* Little, Brown, New York.

LEGAL REFERENCES

61 American Jurisprudence 2d 167 (1981).
61 American Jurisprudence 2d 201 (1981).
Tarasoff v. Regents of the University of California, 529 P.2d 553 (Calif. 1974).

Chapter 3

Issues and Trends in Counseling and Psychotherapy

Issues, or concerns with which there are divergent views, require conceptualization before action can be taken for their resolution. Delineating all the ethical and legal issues inherent in the counseling process would be a monumental task. Indeed, such an endeavor may not serve in promoting understanding, much less conceptualization, or resolution. Nor would it seem productive to identify issues with criticisms, because criticisms of counseling arise from a diverse and confusing host of expectations and from a complex array of functions. The purpose of this chapter, therefore, is to enumerate conceptualizations of issues in counseling with a narrative attempt to stimulate reader discussion and clarity in understanding as a reference point from which resolutions may be achieved and trends can be viewed. Conceptualizations are synthesized under nine major rubrics, in the form of questions, followed by an enumeration of trends. The issues dealt with in this chapter probably suggest author biases, and the trends and future predictions contain an element of crystal ball gazing.

The careful reader of this book will have identified numerous issues concerning the expectations of counseling and its functions in the helping professions. A synthesis of the related legal and ethical content will provide a foundation for conceptualization and a basis on which solutions can be developed.

Counseling—whether seen as a point of view, a process, a set of organized services, or a method for facilitating human learning activities—has become accepted as vital to educational programs in schools and colleges, in agencies, in business, and in industry. The underlying basis for almost universal acceptance is that counseling has come to be thought of as a process of helping individuals examine their life experiences with the goal that they will understand and know themselves and their environment so that purposeful, creative, and effective actions will result (Hansen and Tennyson, 1975).

Various issues and trends in counseling have developed as a result of the origin of their intended services (i.e., school counseling, rehabilitation counseling, mental health counseling); disciplines from which the services are drawn; particular national, state, or local crises; and images practitioners of counseling may create. Even today a particular issue may be shaded by influences of unemployment, economic conditions, needs of special populations, or a particular national, state, or local thrust. It seems as though counseling is in a continual state of flux with issues related to both practitioners and the functions they are expected to perform. The "other" counselor, consultant, or personnel worker continually seems to be the object of search. The "passing parade" of counselors and their "contacts with reality" provide the stuff from which issues are surfaced.

COUNSELING EFFECTIVENESS

In the early fifties, Hans Eysenck raised the question, "Is psychotherapy effective?" (Eysenck, 1952). Later he again raised that question (Eysenck, 1965), as did a former co-worker more recently (Rachman, 1971). Essentially, they found little supporting evidence for any type of psychotherapy in the published literature. A major problem encountered was the lack of adequate studies. Eysenck (1952) found only ten studies with both an acceptable design and acceptable control groups. Certainly this alone is disconcerting evidence for someone intent on finding an empirically validated theory.

Essentially, studies of the effectiveness of psychotherapies found treated subjects improved at a rate similar to control subjects. Although solid figures are lacking, spontaneous remission of symptoms in untreated neurotics is frequent. Some estimates are well over 50 percent (Eysenck, 1965; Rachman, 1971), although figures as low as 30 percent are offered for obsessive-compulsive neurotics (Rachman and Hodgson, 1980) and conduct-disordered children (Patterson, 1980).

Reactions to the aforementioned literature reviews and conclusions have been mixed. Meehl, a statistically oriented psychoanalyst, accepts these dismal conclusions as basically accurate (Meehl, 1966). Similar conclusions have been drawn from a review of psychotherapy with children (Levitt, 1957). Critics have been concerned that unmeasured and subclinical effects have been overlooked (Zetzel, 1966; Kellner, 1966). However, the original conclusion remained. Evidence for the effectiveness of psychotherapy was lacking in the 1960s.

A brief examination of the studies comparing the effects of the different theoretical approaches is in order. The problems associated with empirically testing and comparing theories will be considered to see if studies of global therapy would experience the same shortcomings.

In the investigations of the effectiveness of psychotherapy theories there have been recurring problems. Following are some major problems not only in conducting comparative studies but also in interpreting results:

Lack of adequate control groups
No long-term follow-up
Client dropout rates
Sample selection
Treatment length
Measurement
Overlap of treatment approaches
Rigid adherence to theoretical approaches
Inexperienced therapists

Lack of adequate control groups. Studies comparing the effects of a particular approach often lack adequate control groups. Many investigations indicating a positive effect for a particular theory or technique frequently lack control groups altogether. As indicated, remission of symptoms without treatment is a well-documented phenomena. Certainly some of the purported treatments' effects reflect this.

Control groups used have been inappropriate in other studies. Rogers and Dymond (1954), in an otherwise well-designed study, used a normal control group. The lack of change in the control group should not have been unexpected. If the regression to the mean principle applies, the more pathological the treatment group, the more likely a change toward normal would occur, with or without treatment.

A problem frequently encountered in investigations by psychoanalysts is the lack of random assignment of subjects to treatment and control groups (Rachman, 1971). Such studies are uninterpretable (Campbell and Stanley, 1963).

No long-term follow-up. Extensive follow-up would seem necessary if one is determining the most effective counseling approach. Approaches that enjoy only temporary effects are not of interest. Naturally many studies lack long-term follow-up simply because such studies are aversive to undertake. One does need to know if treatment effects are durable and that treatment groups are superior to control groups at later dates.

Client dropout rates. Clients frequently drop out of therapy before the therapist would wish. Naturally, this occurrence also turns up in studies testing theoretical approaches. However, dropout is not likely to be a random phenomena. For example, Rachman (1971) cites a study with a 80 percent dropout rate. Persons that remained in the study tended to be of high social and economic status.

From a research point of view, dropouts are to either be included in posttests of the group they are in or the study abandoned. Premature termination of therapy, however, does have relevance to global therapy. An approach or technique that suffers from high rates of dropout would be avoided and not incorporated into global therapy.

Treatment length. Comparative studies are often done rather quickly, and the therapy is of a short duration. If therapy is too short, an approach may be deemed ineffective when it in fact is quite effective if used for longer periods of time. There are practical limitations of the length of therapy in most settings, so approaches producing quick results are preferred. Some of the comparative studies have not used equal treatment length for the different approaches. Of course, this disparity also confuses interpretation.

Measurement. Measurement is particularly troublesome in comparative studies. Different approaches wish to measure different variables. Not only is reliability a problem, but determining what measures reflect client improvement is debated. For example, both objective and subjective measures suggesting success may exist, while the clients have not obtained the results they were after.

The use of objective measure such as the Minnesota Multiphasic Personality Inventory (MMPI) are somewhat acceptable. However, many times the sample subjects have scores that are so near the mean that improvement to the mean would not result in a significant improvement statistically.

Overlap of treatment approaches. One comparative study found the behavioral therapists exhibiting qualities such as empathy, warmth, and positive regard to a greater degree than those using person-centered approaches (Sloane et al., 1975). Results are hard to interpret when such occurrences happen. One may assume that within-group variance is greater than between-group variance, so to speak.

Rigid adherence to theoretical approaches. Although overlap of approaches presents research difficulties, the opposite presents problems also. One study compared the effectiveness of systematic desensitization (SD), person-centered therapy, and rational-emotive therapy (RET) (Di Loreto, 1971). Therapists did not deviate from the theoretical approach, even though the SD therapists felt limited by this. Certainly one cannot deal with a wide range of problems with just SD. Interestingly, SD was as effective, if not more so, than the two theoretical approaches being tested.

Inexperienced therapists. Comparative studies have been criticized for employing inexperienced therapists (Ellis, 1971). This is valid criticism if the therapists employed are less skilled than therapists with the same orientation in general. This also assumes that the experienced obtain more results than the inexperienced. Also, for this to be valid criticism, the goal must not be so difficult to learn and employ that few who use it do so appropriately. A parallel is the jet fighter plane so sophisticated that no one can fly it properly.

Since Eysenck's (1965) latest article on the effects of psychotherapy, studies with more positive results have appeared in the literature. Although conclusive results are lacking, the better studies are finding favorable results, event though modest, for most approaches. Di Loreto (1971) found RET, SD, and person-centered therapy to be superior to no treatment. Systematic desensitization appeared to be effective with both introverts and extroverts; the other two approaches were effective with just introverts. Sloane and co-workers (1975) also found positive results for psychotherapy and behavior therapy with a slight edge to the latter.

In summary, based on the research, no counseling approach has demonstrated itself to be superior to other approaches. Bold claims have been made by individual therapists for particular approaches (Wolpe, 1969; Ellis, 1971) but such claims appear premature and biased. To the question "Is psychotherapy effective?, the answer is probably to some extent" (Nelson, 1983, 6).

MALPRACTICE AND UNETHICAL CONDUCT

Malpractice, whether engaged in knowingly or not, is unethical and would be considered so by the courts as well as professional associations. Issues of privacy and confidentiality, client-counselor relationships and responsibility, and client behavior charged to counseling are frequently encountered in contemporary society. The incompetent counselor is in jeopardy with regard to such issues. Frequently, the failure to recognize limitations in training, experience, and competence results in client damage and in charges against the counselor. The implications are obvious. The untrained and incompetent are liable to be seen as unethical and engaging in malpractice. Chapter 5 presents a detailed discussion of malpractice and negligence in counseling.

PROFESSIONAL IDENTITY

Counseling as a helping profession is a fusion of numerous influences. "It brings together the movement toward a more compassionate treatment of mental problems begun in the mid-nineteenth century France, and the psycho-dynamic insights of Freud and psycho-analysis at the turn of this century" (Belkin, 1980, 19). During the past 70 years, counseling has adopted the science of psychometrics and behavioral psychology. It has incorporated the humanistic perspectives of person-centered approaches and the practical insights of cognitive behavior approaches as well as the pragmatic aspects of career and life-span development. The helping professions have experienced a "recent merging of other concerns indigenous to social work" (Belkin, 1980, 17); "the treatment and prevention of child abuse; health counseling; family counseling" (Belkin, 1980, 17); substance abuse, correctional, pastoral, and job counseling; and numerous others. The phenomenal growth and expansion, although well accepted, has not gained a well-established identity, but is seen as a diverse service, provided by many different trained practitioners.

That professional identity is a major issue is supported by the fact that an entire issue of *Counseling Psychologist* (vol. 7, no. 2, 1977) devoted 98 pages, written by leaders in counseling, to finding solutions to the question of professional identity. A picture of the identity issue can be illustrated by a sample of the numerous professional organizations and their representative journals as listed below.

ACPA: American College Personnel Association
Journal of College Student Personnel
ACES: Association for Counselor Education and Supervision
Counselor Education and Supervision
NVGA: National Vocational Guidance Association
Vocational Guidance Quarterly
AHEAD: Association for Humanistic Education and Development
Humanistic Educator
ASCA: American School Counselor Association
School Counselor
Elementary School Guidance and Counseling Journal
ARCA: American Rehabilitation Counseling Association
Rehabilitation Counseling Bulletin
AMEG: Association for Measurement and Evaluation in Guidance
Measurement and Evaluation in Guidance
NECA: National Employment Counselors Association
Journal of Employment Counseling
ANWC: Association for Non-White Concerns in Personnel and Guidance
Journal of Employment Counseling
ARVIC: Association for Religion and Values in Counseling
Counseling and Values
ASWG: Association for Specialists in Group Work
Together
POCA: Public Offender Counselor Association
AMHCA: American Mental Health Counselors Association

In addition to APGA [American Personnel and Guidance Association, as of July 1983, the AACD (American Association for Counseling and Development)], interests of counselors are also represented by The Division of Counseling Psychology of the American Psychology Association. *The Counseling Psychologist,* a prestigious quarterly journal, is published by that division, often organized around specific themes (such as counselor identity, counseling men, etc.). (Belkin, 1980, 47)

COUNSELING VERSUS PSYCHOTHERAPY

The issue of counseling versus psychotherapy has been debated in the literature and at professional conferences for at least four decades. Belkin (1980, 20) boldly declares, "There is no difference." Albert (1966), Ard (1966), Curran (1968), Kirman (1976), and Patterson (1980) tend to agree that the terms are synonymous. The issue, however, is less than agreed upon when legal and ethical questions arise. As Super (1980, 82) explained, "a hitherto somewhat amorphous and debatable field of psychology emerged as clearly a field in its own right . . . merging several streams of development." Those "streams" included "vocational, social differential, and personality psychology and the processes of vocational guidance and psychotherapy" (Pallone, 1977, 29).

Many in the helping professions defend their right to practice counseling in their particular setting, depending on the seriousness of the client's problems, the emotional degree of treatments, and the counselor's training. Indeed, Kirman (1976) found that "from the point of view of the counselor, the differentiation between counseling and psychotherapy becomes meaningless" (p. 84). A counterposition is taken by many—including Aubrey (1967), Bordin (1968), and Blocker (1966)—that counseling and psychotherapy differ depending on the degree of the client's disturbance, the goals of the counseling process, and the level of training of the counselors.

Although the issue remains essentially unresolved, it is clear that a person in the helping professions must be able to define counseling in terms of training, personal competencies, setting, goals, and client's problems. Schmidt (1977, 20) lists five basic assumptions stated in the professional literature that may be used as legal or ethical guidelines for the counselor.

1. The *intent* of counseling is variously described as bringing about change in client's behavior or attitudes and helping clients change or cope with their environment. At times the intent is to help clients to conceptualize their problems, define goals, and to plan meaningful approaches to meeting their goals.
2. The *means* of assisting with intent in bringing about client change is based on theory, research, and learned competencies in counseling methodology.
3. The *responsibility* for change in counseling is usually the client's, based on mutually agreed upon goals by client and counselor.

4. The *setting* or condition under which counseling is practiced is a professional one. This applies whether the counselor is in private practice or is employed by an institution.
5. The *purpose* of counseling is, generally, the improvement or enhancement of the client in his/her existence as opposed to single survival or preservation of life. Nor is the purpose of counseling seen as an attempt to manipulate or restructure a client's personality.

COUNSELOR PREPARATION

Typically counselors are prepared in graduate programs by qualified professional staff. The diversity of training and staff, however, has been at issue for sometime, and it continues to be an issue. In addition to state licensing and credentialing agencies, professional organizations such as the Association for Counselor Education, the American Psychological Association, the American Mental Health Counselor's Association and the National Association of School Psychologists have adopted preparation standards for their members. The following are professional preparation standards of the APGA:

Members who are responsible for training others must be guided by the preparation standards of their association and relevant division(s). The member who functions in the capacity of trainer assumes unique ethical responsibilities that frequently go beyond those of the member who does not function in a training capacity. These ethical responsibilities (*Ethical Standards,* 1981, 4) are outlined as follows:

1. Members must orient students to program expectations, basic skills development, and employment prospects prior to admission to the program.
2. Members in charge of learning experiences must establish programs that integrate academic study and supervised practice.
3. Members must establish a program directed toward developing students' skills, knowledge, and self-understanding, stated whenever possible in competency or performance terms.
4. Members must identify the levels of competencies of their students in compliance with relevant division standards. These competencies must accommodate the paraprofessional as well as the professional.
5. Members, through continual student evaluation and appraisal, must be aware of the personal limitations of the learner that might impede future performance. The instructor must not only assist the learner in securing remedial assistance but also screen from the program those individuals who are unable to provide competent services.
6. Members must provide a program that includes training in research commensurate with levels of role functioning. Paraprofessional and technician-level personnel must be trained as consumers of research. In addition, these personnel must learn how to evaluate their own and their program's effectiveness.

Graduate training, especially at the doctoral level, would include preparation for original research by the member.

7. Members must make students aware of the ethical responsibilities and standards of the profession.
8. Preparatory programs must encourage students to value the ideals of service to individuals and to society. In this regard, direct financial renumeration or the lack of it must not influence the quality of services rendered. Monetary considerations must not be allowed to overshadow professional and humanitarian needs.
9. Members responsible for educational programs must be skilled as teachers and practitioners.
10. Members must present thoroughly varied theoretical positions so that students may make comparisons and have the opportunity to select a position.
11. Members must develop clear policies within their educational institutions regarding field placement and the roles of the student and the instructor in such placement.
12. Members must ensure that forms of learning focusing on self-understanding or growth are voluntary; or if required as part of the education program, are made known to prospective students prior to entering the program. When the education program offers a growth experience with an emphasis on self-disclosure or other relatively intimate or personal involvement, the member must have no administrative, supervisory, or evaluating authority regarding the participant.
13. Members must conduct an educational program in keeping with the current relevant guidelines of the American Personnel and Guidance Association and its divisions.

PROFESSIONAL LICENSING

Professional licensing has become a major issue during the past decade (Fritz and Mills, 1980). Most professional counseling organizations now provide for some type of credentialing for counseling specialists. Leaders among these professional organizations are the American Psychological Association (APA), the American Association for Counseling and Development (AACD), the American Mental Health Counselors Association (AMCHA), the American Association for Marriages and Family Therapy (AAMFT), the American Association of Sex Education, Counselors and Therapists (AASECT), and the Commission on Rehabilitation Counselor Certification (CRCC).

In addition to the ethical considerations incorporated in standards for licensing, support for the need for licensing tends to be based on five arguments (Fritz and Mills, 1980).

First, licensure protects the public by setting and enforcing minimum standards for counselor educators and counseling practitioners. Second, licensing protects consumers who seek professional service. Third, licensure defines counseling services. Fourth, licensure sets standards for training and thereby tends to safeguard against untrained and incompetent practitioners. Fifth, licensure upgrades the profession and serves as a valuable protection in legal matters.

CONFIDENTIALITY AND THE HELPING PROFESSIONS

> Independent of the development of a legal right to privacy and to its derivative right to confidentiality, physicians since the days of Hippocrates have been enjoined (on an ethical basis) from disclosing information they acquire from their patients. "Whatever I shall see or hear in the course of my profession . . . if it be what should not be published abroad, I will never divulge, holding such things to be holy secrets," reads the Hippocratic oath. (Gutheil and Applebaum, 1982)

The helping professions do not have their own "Hippocrates" nor in many cases are they legally protected by statutes that guarantee privileged communication. (See chapter 4.) Only in selected states has the guarantee of confidentiality been established by law.

TRENDS IN THE HELPING PROFESSIONS

Concerns regarding definition of the counseling process and professional identity continue to flourish. The American Personnel and Guidance Association and Division 17 of the American Psychological Association, as well as other professional bodies identified with the helping professions, have been debating these issues since 1952 (Holland, 1982). The trend of discontent in progress and resolution continues.

1. There is a wide range of opinion about our goals and roles. They range from "there is no problem" to vague definitions that encompass large portions of clinical, school, rehabilitation, and industrial psychology. The official divisional definitions are usually unknown to the average member.
2. The label, "counseling psychologist" does not cover the full range of work performed by counseling psychologists. In addition, the label lacks status in the eyes of psychologists and in the eyes of some counseling psychologists and clients.
3. Publications mirror our confusion and disagreement. The *Journal of Counseling Psychology* creates the impression that the counseling relationship represents the main interest and function of our members. Articles about career assistance are in the minority, but surveys indicate that the demand for this kind of help is higher than it is for any other form of assistance (Carney et al., 1979). Several related

> or satellite journals have absorbed much of the research that properly, by some definitions, belongs in the *Journal of Counseling Psychology*. The related journals include the *Journal of Applied Psychology*, the *Vocational Guidance Quarterly*, *Measurement and Evaluation in Guidance*, and others. (Holland, 1982, 7-8)

COUNSELING IN THE MARKETPLACE

Tanney (1982) divides the counseling marketplace into five sections: "health care, college and universities, industry, populations, and political concerns" (p. 21). To these can be added schools, private practice clients, and various government agencies. These marketplace sections support the trend that a growing clientele is being served by the helping professions. Clients of counseling, too, are now including all ages, population differences, and a wider variety of client problems. This trend will continue to demand a professional who is more knowledgeable in legal matters and ethical conduct.

COUNSELING ENCOUNTERS WITH THE JUSTICE SYSTEM

A 1983 issue (vol. 11, no. 2) of *Counseling Psychologist* devoted its entire contents to counseling concerns and trends of counseling in the justice system. Major topics included the criminal justice system, the juvenile justice system, and general issues of counseling service delivery. Editor John M. Whiteley (1983) concluded that the journal issue reports verified the diversity of employment settings and possible populations that are appropriately served by counselors. His recommendations deal with a variety of legal and ethical problems that counselors encounter with the justice system. "With the political and economic uncertainties (funding sources, population variables, legal questions) that we are facing, counseling psychologists should prepare themselves for a pattern of employment, not merely for a specific setting" (Whiteley, 1983, 3). He suggests that "counseling psychologists should familarize themselves with the credentialing requirements of all relevant review panels (AASPB, National Register, etc.) and should insure that they meet the requirements of these groups to guarantee their employment flexibility" (p. 3).

In addition, the National Board for Certified Counselors (National Board for Certified Counselors, 1982) and others have set requirements for counselors. The trend is for more continued credentialing but the issue of definitions and identity continues to persist. Whiteley (1983) suggests that

> training institutions of counseling psychologists should assure that their programs are in keeping with the requirements of the accrediting bodies listed above and should

apprise their students of the potential necessity of meeting these groups' standards (e.g., the requirements for the environments purporting to train psychologists providing health care demand that the trainees be exposed to a heterogeneous professional staff, not just one composed of psychologists). (P. 3)

This recommendation should apply to all training institutions and to all who practice in the helping professions.

The future, as discussed in *Counseling Psychologist* (vol. 8, no. 4, 1980), will see continued growth in the helping professions; and along with growth will be an increased need to clarify legal and ethical matters.

CHAPTER GUIDELINES

1. Major issues in the field of counseling are counseling effectiveness and research accountability on counselor outcomes.
2. Professional identity continues to be an issue as professional standards are proposed, training is assessed, and licensing and/or credentialing is debated.
3. Counseling versus psychotherapy as an issue has not been resolved, but Schmitt's five basic assumptions can be used as a guide to resolve this issue for the individual counselor.
4. Licensure in counseling has become the calling card for the individual profession and will become a requirement for private practice in the future.
5. Trends in the helping profession suggest continued growth, more attention to life-style and career concerns, and increased litigation directed at counselor behavior.

SITUATIONAL DISCUSSIONS

Situation 1: As a practicing counselor, review your own counseling practice with regard to effectiveness. Do you keep records and follow-up data on your clients?

Situation 2: As a professional counselor, write a critique on your professional identity, including your professional affiliation, your work setting, and your personal in-service study.

Situation 3: List and evaluate the professional journals which can be relied upon to provide you with ethical and legal information relevant to your practice.

Situation 4: Identify the opportunity and sources for in-service work for professional counselors in your area.

Situation 5: Conduct a needs analysis on clients you serve with attention to trends that will aid you in planning up-to-date services.

REFERENCES

Albert, G., 1966, If counseling is psychotherapy—what then? *Personnel and Guidance Journal* **45:**124-1-29.

Alexander, D., 1976, Legal issues in guidance, in *School Guidance Services,* T. H. Hohenshil and J. H. Miles, eds., Kendall/Hunt, Dubuque, Iowa, pp. 219-246.

Ard, B., ed., 1966, *Counseling and Psychotherapy,* Science and Behavior Books, New York.

Aubrey, R., 1967, Misapplication of therapy models to school counseling, *Personnel and Guidance Journal* **48:**-273-278.

Belkin, G., 1980, *An Introduction to Counseling,* William C. Brown, Dubuque, Iowa.

Blocker, D., 1966, *Developmental Counseling,* Ronald Press, New York.

Bordin, E., 1968, *Psychological Counseling,* Appleton-Century Crofts, New York.

Campbell, D. T., and J. C. Stanley, 1963, *Experimental and Quasi-Experimental Designs for Research,* Rand McNally, Chicago.

Curran, G., 1968, *Counseling and Psychotherapy,* Sheed and Ward, New York.

Di Loreto, A. O., 1971, *Comparative Psychotherapy and Experimental Analysis,* Aldine and Atherton, New York.

Ellis, A., 1971, RET results, in *Comparative Psychotherapy and Experimental Analysis,* A. O. Di Loreto, ed., Aldine and Atherton, New York, pp. 68-69.

Eysenck, H. J., 1952, The effects of psychotherapy: An evaluation, *Journal of Consulting Psychology* **16:**319-324.

Ethical Standards of the American Personnel and Guidance Association, 1981, Washington, D.C.

Eysenck, H. J., 1952, The effects of psychotherapy: An evaluation, *Journal of Counseling Psychology* **16**:319-324.

Eysenck, H. J., 1965, The effects of psychotherapy, *International Journal of Psychiatry,* **1:**99-142.

Fretz, B., and D. Mills, 1980, *Licensing and Certification of Psychologists and the Law,* Jossey-Bass, San Francisco.

Gutheil, T., and P. Applebaum, 1982, *Clinical Handbook of Psychiatry and the Law,* McGraw-Hill, New York.

Hansen, L. S., and W. W. Tennyson, 1975, A career management model for counselor involvement, *Personnel and Guidance Journal* **53**(9):638-645.

Holland, J., 1982, Planning for alternative futures, *The Counseling Psychologist* **10**(2):7-14.

Kellner, R., 1966, Discussion, in *The Effects of Psychotherapy,* H. J. Eysenck, ed., The International Science Press, New York, p. 86.

Kirman, W., 1976, Emotional education in the classroom: A modern psychoanalytic approach, in *Counseling: Directions and Practice,* G. S. Belkin, ed., Kendall/Hunt, Dubuque, Iowa, pp. 79-92.

Levitt, E. E., 1957, The results of psychotherapy with children, *Journal of Consulting Psychology* **21:**189-196.

Meehl, P. E., 1966, in *The Effects of Psychotherapy,* H. J. Eysenck, ed., The Internal Science Press, New York, pp. 186-199.

National Board For Certified Counselors, Inc., 1982, Certification Application packet, Falls Church, Va.

Nelson, M., 1983, Global Therapy: Techniques and Applications, unpublished paper, Virginia Polytechnic Institute and State University, Blacksburg, Va.

Pallone, N., 1977, Counseling psychology: Toward an emperical definition *Counseling Psychologist* **7:**29-32.

Patterson, C., 1980, *Theories of Counseling and Psychotherapy,* 3rd ed., Harper and Row, New York.

Rachman, S., 1971, *The Effects of Psychotherapy,* Pergamon Press, New York.

Rachman, S., and W. Hodgson, 1980, *Obsessions and Compulsions,* Appleton-Century-Crofts, New York.

Rogers, C. R., and R. F. Dymond, eds., 1954, *Psychotherapy and Personality Change: Coordinated Studies in the Client-Centered Approach,* University of Chicago Press, Chicago.

Schmidt, L., 1977, Why has the professional practice of psychological counseling developed in the United States? *Counseling Psychologist* **7**(2):19-21.

Sloane, R., F. Staples, A. Cristol, N. Yorkston, and K. Whipple, 1975, *Psychotherapy versus Behavior Therapy,* Harvard University Press, Cambridge, Mass.

Super, D., 1980, The year 2000 and all that, *Counseling Psychologist* **8**(4):22-24.

Talbutt, L., and D. Hummel, 1982, Legal and ethical issues impacting on counselors, *Counseling and Human Development* **14**(6):1-12.

Tanney, F., 1982, Counseling psychology and the marketplace, *Counseling Psychologist* **10**(2):21-30.

Whiteley, J., 1980, Counseling psychology in the year 2000 A.D., *Counseling Psychologist* **4**(4):2-7.

Wolpe, J., 1969, *The Practices of Behavior Therapy,* Pergamon Press, New York.

Zetzel, E. R., 1966, Discussion in *The Effects of Psychotherapy,* H. J. Eysenck, ed., The International Science Press, New York, pp. 46-52.

Chapter 4

Confidentiality and Privileged Communication

Counselors, psychologists, and other helping professionals often face ethical decisions about the disclosure of confidential information obtained from clients in the counseling relationship. When and under what circumstances may counselors be required to reveal confidential information? Can counselors be expected to testify in a court of law about information obtained in the counseling session? What are the ethical and legal responsibilities of counselors when the client is a danger to self or society? To better answer these questions, counselors should first understand the terms *confidentiality* and *privileged communication.* Second, counselors should know the status of privileged communication statutes in their states of employment. Third, counselors should understand the implications of those state statutes and court cases for their work settings.

DEFINITIONS AND BACKGROUND

Privileged communication is a legal right granted to certain professionals not to testify in a court of law regarding confidential information obtained in their professional relationship. Confidentiality, on the other hand, has most

Selected portions of this chapter are used with permission from L. C. Talbutt and D. Hummel, 1982, Legal issues impacting on counselors, *Counseling and Human Development* **14**(6):1-12.

often been described as an ethical decision not to reveal what is learned in the professional relationship. Litwack, Rochester, Oates, and Addison (1969) explained that privileged communication and confidentiality have often been defined the same way in professional literature, even though the two terms are different. They wrote, "Privileged communication refers to the right of the counselor to refuse to divulse any confidential information while testifying in a court of law" (p. 108). Confidentiality, an ethical term, "refers to a professional's decision . . . not [to] divulge what has been revealed . . . in his contact with a client" (p. 108). Marsh and Kinnick (1970) gave similar definitions. They defined privilege communication "as the immunity from criminal and/or civil action for what one says or refuses to say" and confidentiality as "a quasi-legal term to describe the status of communication as being privileged" (pp. 363-364).

Confidentiality has an important ethical meaning for counselors. Chase (1976) wrote, "The right to privacy is basic not only in maintaining a democracy, but also in preserving human dignity" (p. 331). Counselors always have an ethical obligation to maintain a client's confidentiality unless the client or others are in danger or unless there is a legal requirement to testify in a court of law. "The Ethical Principles of Psychologists" (1981) states the following regarding confidentiality:

> Psychologists have a primary obligation to respect the confidentiality of information obtained from persons in the course of their work as psychologists. They reveal such information to others only with the consent of the person or the person's legal representative, except in those unusual circumstances in which not to do so would result in clear danger to the person or to others. (pp. 633-634)

Clearly psychologists are bound to maintain confidentiality unless the client or others are in danger or the client or the client's legal representative have given consent for disclosure. Pietrofesa and Vriend (1971) explained that ethical counseling requires confidentiality (p. 107). Even in the absence of privilege communication statutes, they maintain that counselors should follow ethical practices in their work.

Privileged communication originated in common law through customs and rulings of the courts, but it has been expanded through legislative bodies. Burgum and Anderson (1975) explained that common law originally allowed privileged communication in only two relationships: husband-wife and attorney-client. However, they reported that legislative groups have expanded that privilege to "such relationships as clergyman and penitent, reporter and informer, doctor and patient, and psychologist and client" (p. 14). Counselors in a number of states also have been granted privileged communication by statutes. Both the courts and professional literature indicate that in the absence of state legislation, counselors can probably be required to testify in court about information obtained in the counseling relationship.

The two types of privileged communication are absolute and conditional. Marsh and Kinnick (1970) defined absolute privileged communication as "unconditional," which can be granted "only by legislative or constitutional action" (p. 363). Absolute privileged communication does not require that certain conditions be met in order to exist. However, it "exists only with respect to the official proceedings of legislative and judicial agencies" (p. 363). Conditional privileged communication means that things such as "absence of malice, fair comment, and official status" must be present, with the courts determining if these conditions have been met (p. 363). Marsh and Kinnick (1970) and Denkowski and Denkowski (1982) believe that privileged communication laws for counselors and mental health practitioners are conditional, not absolute.

Privileged communication exists for clients, not counselors. Thus, clients can waive their rights. Boyd and Heinsen (1971) wrote, "Privilege itself is basically an extension of the Fifth Amendment privilege and, hence is not the professional's, but the client's" (p. 227). Privileged communication has developed because of the need for justice on one hand and the individual's need for privacy on the other. McDermott (1974) explained the reasons for the existence of privileged communication.

> The nature of any particular physical or emotional anguish may be so intimate, suggestive or potentially injurious that disclosure of the facts would subject the citizen to undue pain, loss of stature and injury to reputation. The citizen would be most reluctant to engage in relationships with the helping professions if the intimacies of his private life were vulnerable to disclosure before the entire public. (P. 25)

McDermott concluded that some relationships are so valuable that state laws have exempted certain professionals, such as attorneys, priests, physicians, and psychologists, from testifying about those relationships.

STATUS OF PRIVILEGED COMMUNICATION FOR COUNSELORS

Privileged communication statutes for counselors have increased dramatically in recent years. In a national survey for the Privileged Communication Committee of the American School Counselor Association, Litwack (1975) found that 12 states offered privileged communication for school counselors as opposed to only 2 states in 1968 (pp. 194–195). Alexander (1976) reported that 15 states offered privileged protection to counselors (p. 229). Those states were Connecticut, Delaware, Idaho, Indiana, Maine, Michigan, Montana, Nevada, North Carolina, North Dakota, Oklahoma, Oregon, Pennsylvania, South Dakota, and Kentucky (p. 243). More recently Denkowski and Denkowski (1982) found that 20 states offer school counselors confidentiality (p. 372). Their investigation revealed that state laws differ in the degree of protection for clients. For example, some states grant counselors privileged communication in criminal and civil cases, while other laws grant only privileged communication for civil cases. Denkowski and Denkowski (1982) also found that other professionals such as mental health personnel have often been granted privileged communication rights by state licensing laws. They predict that in the future all mental health practitioners will be granted privileged communication.

Virginia is an example of a state that has recently granted privileged communication rights to licensed professional counselors. The law grants privileged communication to licensed professional counselors, social workers, and psychologists in civil cases, not criminal proceedings. Also, the Virginia code does not extend the statute in child abuse matters when the "physical or mental condition of the client is at issue" or when "a court, in the exercise of sound disgression, deems such disclosure necessary to the proper administration of justice" (Virginia Annotated Code, 1982). The law does not name school counselors or clerical workers who maintain school records.

By comparison, another state grants privileged communication to teachers, guidance officers, clerical workers, and others in both civil or criminal actions (Complied Laws of the State of Michigan, 1963). When state laws on privileged communication exist, they vary in strength and differ in the professionals that are named.

Virginia was cited earlier as a state that recently granted privileged communication rights to licensed professional counselors in civil cases (not criminal cases). The following discussion of a Virginia court case illustrates the thinking of the court prior to the recently passed statute. In a criminal case *Gibson v. Commonwealth* (1975, with writ of Certiorari denied by the U.S. Supreme Court 1976), the Virginia Supreme Court upheld a lower court decision to allow a psychiatrist to testify regarding a client's admission of guilt to a crime. The court found that the psychiatrist's testimony did not violate the physician-patient privilege statute. The following explanation was given: "There exists, however, no physician-patient privilege in a criminal prosecution in Virginia. The common law recognized no such privilege in either civil or criminal proceedings . . . While Virginia has enacted a statutory privilege, it is expressly confined to civil proceedings" (*Gibson v. Commonwealth,* 1975, 847). Clearly, physicians in Virginia did not possess statutory privileged communication rights in criminal proceedings. Thus, it was logical to expect that when or if legislation was passed in Virginia for professional counselors, it would be limited to civil cases. Counselors in states without privileged communication would be wise to examine the status of laws for other similar professionals to get a feel for the philosophy of their state. States that limit privileged communication for physicians would likely place consistent limitations on other professionals.

An examination of the following questions should help counselors better understand their state's privileged communication statute:

Does the state in which you are employed have a specific law granting privileged communication to counselors? If not, counselors would likely be required to testify in a court of law.

Does the law name school counselors, clerical staff who manage records, psychologists, licensed professional counselors, social workers, or others?

Does the law grant the privilege in civil cases, criminal cases, or both?

Does the state law list exceptions such as child abuse matters, or matters when a client's mental health is an issue?

Does the law state that the court may waive the privilege when it deems the professional's testimony necessary for fairness and justice?

Answers to these questions should help counselors assess their state's statutes on privileged communication.

IMPLICATIONS OF COURT CASES FOR COUNSELORS

Ware (1964) wrote that the courts generally use Wigmore's four fundamental conditions to determine whether a communication should be privileged (p. 3). For example, in *Mullen v. United States* (1958), the court ruled that a confession made to a Lutheran minister was privileged communication and was inadmissible in court because the relationship between the penitent and minister met Wigmore's four conditions for privileged communication.

(1) The communication must originate in a *confidence* that they will not be disclosed;
(2) This element of *confidentiality must be essential* to the full and satisfactory maintenance of the relation between the parties;
(3) The *relation* must be one which in the opinion of the community ought to be sedulously *fostered;* and

(4) The *injury* that would inure to the relation by the disclosure of the communications must be *greater than the benefit* thereby gained for the correct disposal of litigation. (*Mullen v. U.S.*, 1958, 280)

The following case also cited Wigmore, and used some slightly different language to describe the conditions necessary for privileged communication to exist. In *Cimijatti v. Paulsen* (1963), the Northern District court of Iowa overruled a motion to compel a clergyman to testify regarding the communication from a penitent and explained that the necessary conditions for privileged communication had been met. They were

1. That the statements are made in the usual course of the discipline
2. That the person claiming the privilege is allowed by the statute to claim it
3. That the communication was secret
4. That the statements are penitential in character and made by the penitent. (P. 624)

There are exceptions recognized by the courts even when privileged communication statutes exist. *Whalen v. Roe* (1977), a United States Supreme Court case, determined that a New York law requiring physicians to give the state copies of certain drug prescriptions was constitutional. In its ruling the court offered the following explanation about privileged communication: "Physician-patient evidentiary privilege is unknown to the common law; in states where it exists by legislative enactment it is subject to many exceptions and to waiver for many reasons" (p. 870).

Generally, a person claiming privileged communication would have the burden of showing that the relationship is covered by the statute. In *Matter of Moser* (1976), the Court of Appeals of Oregon affirmed a lower court decision that the psychologist, a consultant for juvenile court, could testify regarding an evaluation of the mother in question because the psychologist considered his role for the agency as one of evaluation rather than treatment. The court stated the following: "Persons asserting psychologist-client privilege have burden of showing both that such person and nature of testimony offered are within ambit of statute according the privilege" (p. 1022).

Some states have allowed the courts discretion in interpreting privileged communication statutes. The Court of Appeals of North Carolina upheld a lower court ruling in *State v. Bryant* (1969), which allowed a physician to testify regarding the intoxication level of a defendant. The North Carolina statute grants patient and physician privileged communication rights but allows the judge to request disclosure if in the judge's opinion, it is necessary "for the proper administration of justice" (p. 842). The court cited the following example of discretion:

Our Legislature intended the statute to be a shield and not a sword. It was careful to make provision to avoid injustice and suppression of truth by putting it in the power of the trial judge to compel disclosure. Judges should not hesitate to require the disclosure where it appears to them to be necessary in order that the truth be known and justice be done. (P. 846)

Privileged communication statutes usually are strictly construed by the courts, meaning that the courts will not grant the privileges unless a professional is granted privileged communication by state law. In *United States v. Jaskiewisez* (1968), the Eastern District court of Pennsylvania decided that without a statute, no accountant-client privilege existed. The Ohio State Supreme court in *Arnovitz v. Wogar* (1964) also ruled that privileged communication statutes are strictly construed. The court stated that statutes making certain communications priviledged "are in derogation of the common law and should be strictly construed" (p. 665). In *Davision v. St. Fire & Marine Ins. Co.* (1977), the Supreme Court of Wisconsin made the following point regarding privilege communication: "If sought-after privilege arises from the common law, it must be adopted either by Supreme Court rule or by statute, and not on a case-by-case basis" (p. 435). In a similar case in the Wisconsin State Supreme court, the judge in *State v. Driscoll* (1972), asked to grant privileged communication for social workers, offered the following conclusion: "It is for the legislature, not the courts, to determine whether communications between social workers and those they serve or counsel are to be privileged" (p. 858).

The courts have generally held that unless professionals have been granted privileged communication by statute, none exists. For example, if a particular state law grants privileged communication to licensed professional counselors but does not name social workers or school guidance counselors, the court decisions indicate that the courts would follow the exact wording of the law rather than expand the statute to social workers and school counselors. Social workers, school counselors, or others would need to seek their own legislation if not named in an existing statute. Also, court decisions have revealed that privileged communication statutes are often subject to waivers and exceptions even when statutes exist. The courts must examine the need for testimony for fairness and justice against the need for professional-client privacy.

No Absolute Privacy Right

The United States Supreme Court has maintained that there is no absolute privacy right. The Court stated in *Katz v. U.S.* (1967) there is "no general constitutional right to privacy" (p. 350). More recently in *Roe v. Wade* (1973), it noted that "the Constitution does not explicitly mention any right of privacy" (p. 152). According to *Roe,* as far back as 1891, the Supreme Court has recognized certain privacy rights under the First, Fourth, Fifth,

Ninth, and Fourteenth amendments. These rights include activities related to marriage, contraception, family relationships, and similar matters (pp. 152-153). In *Roe* the Court concluded that "the right of personal privacy includes the abortion decision" (p. 154). However, *Whalen v. Roe* (1977) indicated that the United States Supreme Court did not recognize the doctor-patient relationship as a privacy right covered by the Constitution. The following case represents a similar legal point of view and has implications for counselors, psychologists, and others in the helping professions.

In *Felber v. Foote* (1970, p. 85) the U.S. District court concluded that privileged communication between physician and patient is "afforded solely by laws of individual states and there is no federal constitutional right to such privilege." In that particular case, the psychiatrist, in the absence of a statutory privilege, was required to report names of drug-dependent persons to the Commissioner of Health. This case suggests to medical and other helping professions that privileged communication exists only if it is granted by statute.

Tort Cases Involving Privileged Communication

The courts have addressed the doctrine of absolute privilege claimed by defendants in tort cases involving physicians and psychotherapists. The two defenses used in tort cases (defined in chapter 5), truth and absolute privilege, are discussed in the chapter on libel and slander. However, this section includes some examples of court cases involving physicians and psychotherapists who have claimed absolute privilege in tort cases. In *Re Lifschutz* (1970), the Supreme Court of California ruled that psychiatrists do not possess absolute privilege concerning psychotherapeutic communication rights and that a limited disclosure of the psychotherapist-patient relationship may be allowed in court when justified. This case was concerned with a plaintiff who brought an assault charge for physical and mental distress. During the court action, the plaintiff indicated that he had previously received psychiatric treatment. The defendant, then, subpoenaed the psychiatrist and his records. The psychiatrist refused to answer questions or to produce the records. The court recognized a limited waiver in order to reveal information relevant to the case. Dr. Lifschutz claimed that the California constitution gave him an absolute right to protect the confidential relationship, regardless of the patient's wishes (p. 561). Recognizing that psychiatrists do not possess absolute privilege, the court stated, "We do not believe the patient-psychotherapist privilege should be frozen into the rigidity of absolutism" (p. 573).

In *Caesar v. Mountanos* (1976), the California Circuit Court ruled that when a patient "placed 'mental or emotional condition' in issue," the patient waives the patient-psychotherapist privilege. The court summarized its view in the following ruling: "[T]he Supreme Court of California in *Lifschutz* strikes a proper balance between the conditional right of privacy encompassing the psychotherapist-patient relationship and the state's compelling need to insure the ascertainment of the truth in court proceedings" (p. 1070).

Yoho v. Lindsley (1971), a negligence case, stated that when a patient brings action in which mental ailments are an issue, there is no longer reason for privileged communication. However, the Fourth District Court of Appeal in Florida determined that the psychotherapist should only answer questions related to the "subject matter of this action" (p. 189). The court gave the following explanation:

> The whole purpose of the [physician-patient] privilege is to preclude the humiliation of the patient that might follow disclosure of his ailments. When the patient himself discloses those ailments by bringing an action in which they are in issue, there is no longer any reason for the privilege. (P. 191)

Also, in *United States Ex Rel. Edney v. Smith* (1976), the U.S. District Court of New York court ruled that by claiming insanity the defendant waived any claim of privileged communication. The court explained that the psychotherapist-patient privilege is qualified, not absolute, and that in some situations the defendent, either by "actual or implied" waiver, justifies a disclosure (p. 1039). In a similar case, *State v. Aucoin* (1978), the State Supreme Court of Louisiana held that when a defendant claims mental health to be an issue, the admission of evidence by the psychiatrist does not violate the psychiatrist-patient privilege.

Recently a court ruling emphasized another area in which the physician-patient privilege may be lost. Privileged communication rights do not prevent doctors and psychotherapists from their duty to warn others when they are in danger. In *Tarasoff v. Regents of University of California* (1974) the Supereme Court of California determined that a doctor or psychotherapist has a responsibility to warn threatened persons when they may be harmed. Although this case will be covered more thoroughly in the chapter on civil liability, the court addressed the issue of privacy as well. The court explained that "[t]he protective privilege ends where the public peril begins" (p. 561). In other words, when the client is a threat to self or others, the counselor must take action by informing the proper authorities or person in danger. The ruling in *Tarasoff* displays thinking similar to that revealed in *Ethical Standards* (1981).

> When the client's condition indicates that there is clear and imminent danger to the client or others, the member must take reasonable personal action or inform

responsible authorities. Consultation with other professionals must be used where possible. The assumption of responsibility for the client(s) behavior must be taken only after careful deliberation. The client must be involved in the resumption of responsibility as quickly as possible. (*Ethical Standards*, 1981, 2)

GROUP COUNSELING

Group counseling presents special problems regarding confidentiality. Burgum and Anderson (1975) reported that some jurisdictions have ruled that the presence of a third party has meant that privileged communication has been lost to all parties involved (pp. 22-24). Burgum and Anderson advised counselors to avoid discussions about criminal acts in the group process unless clients wish to take the risk after having been informed about the status of confidentiality. Van Hoose and Kottler (1978) suggested that group leaders, even more than counselors for individuals, have an ethical duty to discuss with clients the basic rules for group counselors (p. 139). Previously mentioned cases have suggested that statutes dealing with privileged communication will be strictly construed by the courts and that unless rights are specifically stated, the courts will not recognize them. The courts have ruled that privileged communication may be lost, even in established confidential relationships (such as husband and wife) when third parties are present. In *Wolfe v. United States* (1933), the United States Supreme Court determined that husband and wife communications conducted in the presence of a third party were not privileged. Then, in *Perira v. U.S.* (1974), the United States Supreme Court ruled, "The presence of a third party . . . negatives presumption of privacy" (p. 358).

Olson (1971, 288) recommended that counselors for groups should follow the ethical standards of the American Psychological Association and the American Personnel and Guidance Association as well as professional standards designed for group work (p. 288). Regarding confidentiality Olson (1971, 288) suggested:

> The leader must safeguard information that has been obtained in his work with groups. While the leader can vouch only for his own respect for confidentiality in the group, he must inform the members of the group of their responsibility for confidentiality and also make them aware that he cannot speak for anyone other than himself.

Davis (1980) found in a survey of group counseling members and leaders that a group leader's presentation or discussion of confidentiality significantly affected members' actions and thoughts about confidentiality (p. 199). Davis suggested that group leaders should discuss their role regarding confidentiality. Also, he recommended that group leaders have a responsibility to discuss with members expectations regarding confidentiality.

In the first session, as the leader and members discuss rules of behavior, the leader can give examples of who the members may talk to and what they may talk about.... A discussion about the consequences of violations of confidentiality or trust ... could ensue or be initiated by the leader. (P. 201)

Davis reported that this procedure might enhance confidentiality but could not ensure it. Thus, confidentiality may not be realistic in group counseling. Finally, Davis recommended that group leaders present an accurate description of confidentiality in order for group members to decide upon their desired involvement in group counseling (1980, p. 201).

The American School Counselor Association ("ASCA Position Statements," 1983) and *Ethical Standards* (1981) addressed confidentiality for group work. The ASCA specified: "Counselors should be aware that it is much more difficult to guarantee confidentiality in group counseling than in individual counseling" (1983). In section B-2, the *Ethical Standards* (1981, 1) requires that "the counseling relationship and information resulting therefrom be kept confidential, consistent with the obligations of the member as a professional person. In a group counseling setting, the counselor must set a norm of confidentiality regarding all group participants' disclosures." Section B-6 *Ethical Standards,* 1981, 2) states that "use of data derived from a counseling relationship for purposes of counselor training as a research shall be confined to content that can be sufficiently disguised to ensure full protection of the identity of the subject client."

Here are some helpful recommendations for counselors regarding group counseling and confidentiality.

1. Counselors should discuss "confidentiality" with the group in terms of the member's role and the counselor's role. This discussion could take place in both prescreening and early sessions.
2. Counselors should continue to remind the group about confidentiality throughout group sessions.
3. Counselors should remind the group to maintain confidentiality even when the group ceases to meet.
4. Counselors might have clients enter into an agreement regarding group confidentiality. The agreement could spell out actions when confidentiality is not maintained.
5. Counselors might discuss certain state or federal laws significant to the interest of the group. For example, in drug counseling, counselors might discuss certain laws in early sessions so clients know both the laws and risks involved in group counseling.
6. Counselors should encourage group members to confront other members not following standards of confidentiality. Such discussions should be handled within the group.

CHILDREN AND CONFIDENTIALITY

Another difficult area for counselors concerns the rights of parents versus the rights of children regarding confidential information. When should parents, for example, be informed regarding the contents of the counseling session? Even, should they ever be informed?

Wagner (1981) conducted a study to compare the attitudes of elementary, middle, and secondary school counselors' attitudes regarding the practice of confidentiality. The results of Wagner's study revealed that secondary school counselors showed the greatest endorsement of confidentiality, with elementary school counselors showing the least endorsement. As clients get older, then, counselors are more likely to subscribe to confidentiality (Wagner, 1981, 306).

Wagner (1981, 310) recommended that children and youth should control confidential information with the following exceptions: when clients waive the right to free choice, when child abuse is involved, or when the child is a threat to self or others (the latter includes suicide intent or attempts). In Wagner's judgment if counselors feel that parents should be involved, the counseling focus should shift from child to family counseling (p. 310).

The school counselor, more than counselors in other settings, is most often faced with conflicts about minors. This situation is especially true for elementary and middle school counselors whose entire client population is made up of minors. Zingaro (1983) reported three situations in which counselors must break confidentiality: when the client requests it, when not to do so would result in clear danger to the client or others, when the courts request it (p. 264).

Zingaro (1983, 265-266) suggested seven guidelines for counselors working with children. They are briefly summarized.

1. Child client and counselor communications are confidential.
2. Case material should not be discussed with persons not involved in the case.
3. In making reports counselors should only present data germane to the report.
4. When the client may harm self or others, the counselor should talk to the client about discontinuing the activity, explain the counselor's responsibility, and then, if steps one and two fail, take appropriate action or inform the proper authorities.
5. If subpoenaed to testify, a counselor might consider becoming an agent of the client's attorney, who could request that the testimony be privileged or made in the judge's chambers. "Neither of these options guarantees" privileged communication.
6. When a counselor is unsure of proper actions, other professionals should be contacted.

7. When parents or others request information, counselors might respond by telling them what to do or not to do to help the child. Zingaro (1983) reported that this approach helps the child and maintains confidentiality too.

An examination of the recommendations offered by Wagner and Zingaro are consistent with the rest of the chapter. Counselors should maintain confidentiality with clients. There are simply more pressures placed on counselors to disregard the confidentiality of underage clients.

CHAPTER GUIDELINES

1. Privileged communication is a legal right granted by statute; confidentiality is a professional and ethical decision to maintain confidential information.
2. Counselors have ethical responsibilities to maintain confidential information regardless of whether or not their state has a privileged communication statute. Exceptions are made when the counselor has legal obligations or when there is danger to the client or others. The literature, professional ethical standards, and the courts are consistent on this issue. Alexander (1976) wrote that there are times when the school counselor, as "an arm of the administration," must put the welfare of other students over that of the counselee (p. 227). The APGA *Ethical Standards* (1981, 2) states, "When the client's condition indicates . . . danger to the client or others, the member must take reasonable personal action."
3. In states that do not have privileged communication statutes for counselors, it is highly likely that they would have to testify regarding confidential information obtained through a counseling session.
4. Counselors in states desiring privileged communication should lobby for state legislation. However, counselors should note that even when privileged communication statutes exist, they may be limited and are subject to court interpretations.
5. Privileged communication is the client's right. Thus, clients may waive that right and request the release of confidential information.
6. Group counseling presents problems regarding confidentiality. Counselors should follow their professional standards as well as ethical standards designed for group work.

SITUATIONAL DISCUSSIONS

Situation 1: As a school or agency counselor, what are your obligations to reveal confidential information when students or other members in the setting are in danger from the client(s)? Explain the counselor's legal and ethical responsibilities. Determine if appropriate guidelines for this situation exist in professional standards.

Situation 2: As a professional counselor, write a summary statement appropriate for your clients defining your ethical and legal responsibilities regarding confidentiality and privileged communication.

Situation 3: Identify five or six common ground rules concerning confidentiality appropriate for any group counseling setting.

Situation 4: Children have rights regarding confidentiality. Make several recommendations helpful for counselors working with children regarding confidentiality.

Situation 5: Determine if the state where you work as a counselor has a privileged communication law. If so, analyze it in terms of professionals included and limitations.

REFERENCES

Alexander, David, 1976, Legal issues in guidance, in *School Guidance Services,* T. H. Hohenshil and J. H. Miles, eds., Kendal/Hunt, Dubuque, Iowa, pp.219-246.

ASCA position statements, 1983, *The ASCA Counselor* **20:**1-8.

Boyd R. E., and R. D. Heinsen, 1971, Problems in privileged communication, *Personnel and Guidance Journal* **50:**276-279.

Burgum, T., and S. Anderson, 1976, *The Counselor and the Law,* APGA Press, Washington, D.C.

Chase, C., 1976, Classroom testing and the right to privacy, *Phi Delta Kappan* **58:**331-332.

Davis, K. L., 1980, Is confidentiality in group counseling realistic? *Personnel and Guidance Journal* **59:**197-201.

Denkowski, K., and G. Denkowski, 1982, Client-counselor confidentiality: An update of rationale, legal status and implications, *Personnel and Guidance Journal* **60:**371-375.

Ethical principles of psychologists, 1981, *American Psychologist* **36:**633-638.

Ethical Standards, American Personnel and Guidance Association, 1981, Washington, D.C.

Litwack, L., 1975, Testimonial privileged communication: A problem reexamined, *The School Counselor* **22:**194-196.

Litwack, L., D. Rochester, R. Oates, and W. Addison, 1969, Testimonial privileged communication and the school counselor, *The School Counselor* **17:**108-111.

McDermott, P. A., 1974, Law and the school psychologist: Privileged communication, malpractice and liability, *School Psychology Digest* **3**(25):27.

Marsh, J. J., and B. C. Kinnick, 1970, Let's close the confidentiality gap, *Personnel and Guidance Journal* **48:**362-365

Olson, L. C., 1971, Ethical standards for group leaders, *Personnel and Guidance Journal* **50:**288.

Pietrofesa, F., and F. Vriend, 1971, *The School Counselor as a Professional,* F. E. Peacock, Itasca, Ill.

Van Hoose, W. H., and J. Kottler, *Ethical and Legal Issues in Counseling and Psychotherapy,* Jossey-Bass, San Francisco.

Wagner, C. A., 1981, Confidentiality and the school counselor, *Personnel and Guidance Journal* **59:**305-310.

Ware, M. L., 1964, *Law of Guidance and Counseling,* W. H. Anderson, Cincinnati.

Zingaro, J. C., 1983, Confidentiality: To tell or not to tell, *Elementary School Guidance and Counseling* **70:**362-367.

LEGAL REFERENCES

Arnovitz v. Wogar, 222 N.E.2d 66 (S.C. Ohio 1964).

Caesar v. Mountanos, 542 F.2d 1064 (Calif. Cir. 1976).

Cimijatti v. Paulsen, 219 F. Supp. 621 (N.D. Iowa 1963).

Compiled Laws of the State of Michigan 600.2165-2166 (1963).

Davision v. St. Fire & Marine Ins. Co., Wis., 248 N.W.2d 433 (S.C. Wis. 1977).

Felber v. Foate, 321 F. Supp. 85 (D. Conn. 1970).

Gibson v. Commonwealth Va., 219 S.E.2d 845 (1975); 425 U.S. 994 (1976).

Katz v. U.S., 398 U.S. 479 (1967).

Matter of Moser, 554 P.2d 1022 (Or. Cir. 1976).

Mullen v. U.S., 263 F.2d 275 (1958).

Perira, v. U.S., 74 S.Ct. 358 (1974).

Re Lifschutz, 467 P.2d 557 (S.C. Calif. 1970).

Roe v. Wade, 410 U.S. 113 (1973)

State v. Aucoin, 362 So.2d 503 (S.C. La. 1978).

State v. Bryant 167 S.E.2d 841 (N.C. Cir. 1969).

State v. Driscoll, 193 N.W.2d 851 (S.C. Wis. 1972).

Tarasoff v. Regents of University of Calif., 529 P.2d 553 (S.C. Calif. 1974).

U.S. Ex Rel. Edney v. Smith, 425 F. Supp. 1038 (E.D. N.Y. 1976).

U.S. v. Jaskiewisez, 178 F. Supp. 525 (E.D. Pa. 1968)

Virginia Code Ann. 8.01-400.2 (1982).

Whalen v. Roe, 97 S.Ct. 869 (1977).

Wolfe v. U.S., 54 S.Ct. 279 (1933).

Yoho v. Lindsley, 248 So.2d 187, (4th., Fla. 1971).

Chapter 5

Civil Liability

Burgum and Anderson (1975, 25) wrote that civil liability means a person can be sued "for not doing right or for doing wrong to another." Counselors, psychologists, psychotherapists, and other professionals are expected to follow certain professional, ethical, and legal standards of conduct in their work. When they do not, litigation may result. Litigation may fall into two categories, common torts and constitutional torts. Common tort comes from the Latin *torquere* meaning "to twist." The basic concept of tort, which comes from old English law, is that each individual has a legal and social obligation to protect other individuals in society. If one person breaches or twists the relationship and someone is injured, then the injured party may sue and be compensated for the injury. The injured party has been diminished; and the only means we have, as a society, to make the person whole again is through a monetary settlement. The common tort is applicable to professionals whether they are in private practice or are employees of a government body.

Alexander, Corns, and McCann (1969) defined torts as "any civil wrong independent of contract" and summarized:

> The law also grants to each individual certain personal rights not of a contractual nature, such as freedom from personal injury and security of life, liberty, and

Selected portions of this chapter are used with permission from L. C. Talbutt and D. Hummel, 1982, Legal issues impacting on counselors, *Counseling and Human Development* **14**(6):1-12.

property. The law imposes corresponding duties and responsibilities on each individual to respect these rights of others. If, by speech or other conduct, we fail to respect these rights, thereby damaging another individual, we have committed a tort and may be held financially liable for our action. (P. 324)

Although the foundation for constitutional torts is old, the litigation in this area is of more recent origin and is still being defined by the courts. The basic concept, which applies only to public officials, extends liability to those officials who, in their official capacity, violate the statutory or constitutional rights of an individual. If a statutory or constitutional violation transpires, then the public official may be held personally liable.

COMMON TORTS

While this chapter discusses both common and constitutional torts, common torts are applicable to professionals in both the private and public sectors. Common torts may be divided into three areas: international interference with an individual, strict liability, and negligence.

Intentional interference. An individual may be liable where the act was intentional and resulted in injury. The intentional act may be malicious or no more than a good-natured joke. The basic premise is that one acts and knowingly continues to act and injury is sustained by a party. Intentional torts cover assault; battery; defamation, including the twin torts of libel and slander; and interference with peace of mind. An example of a commonly litigated intentional tort is that of corporal punishment where a child is paddled and is injured in the process.

Strict liability. When an injury occurs from an act that was not intentional and did not involve negligence, fault is imposed because someone must be held responsible for the injury. Consequently, strict liability applies when someone is injured as a result of the creation of a dangerous situation. Few such cases are found in the area of the helping professions. Because most professionals do not create dangerous situations, most cases against professionals are either torts of intentional interference or negligence.

Negligence. Alexander, Corns, and McCann (1969) described an act of negligence as "neither expected nor intended" but one in which a reasonable man could have "anticipated the harmful results" (p. 693). The reasonable "man" (person) has been described in the courts "as an ideal" or model of conduct and a community standard (p. 694). For negligence to exist, four elements must be present.

1. A *duty* on the part of the actor to protect others;
2. A *failure* on the part of the actor to exercise an appropriate standard of care;
3. The act must be the *proximate* cause or *legal cause* of the injury;
4. An *injury,* causing damage or loss, must exist. (P. 695)

Malpractice

Malpractice in counseling can be defined as harm to a client resulting from professional negligence, with *negligence* defined as the departure from acceptable professional standards. Van Hoose and Kottler (1978) defined malpractice as "damage to another person as a result of negligence" (p. 96) and negligence "as a departure from usual practice; that is, acceptable standards were not followed and due care was not exercised" (p. 97). They reported that counselor malpractice lawsuits are few compared to those of physicians, but they believe this trend will change. They believe that malpractice in counseling would likely follow the same standards used in medical malpractice because guidelines for counselors are not clearly established (Van Hoose and Kottler, 1978, p. 98). Burgum and Anderson (1975) also agreed that malpractice against counselors is unclear (p. 34).

Talbutt and Hummel (1982, 8) identified the following danger areas for counselors: falling below conduct appropriate to one's profession; failing to warn or take action when someone is in danger; taking advantage of the counseling relationship for personal gain; and advising beyond one's skill and training. Slimak and Berkowitz (1983) identified six potential areas for malpractice suits against mental health practitioners:

1. Faulty diagnosis; that is, diagnosis of a problem of physical origin as psychological;
2. Improper certification in a commitment proceeding;
3. Failure to exercise adequate precautions for a suicidal patient;
4. Breach of confidentiality;
5. Faulty applications of therapy; and
6. Promise of a cure, which may form the basis of a breach of contract. (Pp. 291-292)

Burgum and Anderson observed that counselors are judged by standards suitable to their profession and examined potential legal problems when a client fails to make progress or when the professional uses ineffective techniques (1975, 33-34). Similar to the medical field and based on the court case *Johnston v. Rodis* (1958), Burgum and Anderson believe that counselors who act in good faith or make the kind of error any "careful and skillful" counselor could make (p. 34) would not be liable for a client's lack of progress. However, Burgum and Anderson warned counselors that they are responsible for referring clients when the problem is beyond the counselor's skill and training (p. 35). Counselors were also advised against going beyond their professional scope in such areas as dispensing drugs and medicine (Burgum and Anderson, 1975, 56).

Guerrieri v. Tyson (1942) is an example of liability charges. Three public school teachers went beyond their skill and training when they treated the infected finger of a student by placing it in boiling water, which resulted in permanent disfigurement of the student's hand. The Pennsylvania Superior court ruled in favor of the student and found the teachers liable for damages. All counselors, licensed professional, or school counselors, should limit their responsibilities to their own profession and not enter into a field beyond their training and knowledge.

Burgum and Anderson (1975) believed that many common torts in public schools arise because of negligence in the area of supervision. "Disturbed" or "incapacitated" students should not be dismissed from counseling and be allowed to return to their destination without assistance (p. 32). They concluded, "The counselor should do what any reasonable prudent person would do" (p. 33). They also recommend certain standards for group counseling. The counselor should "(1) attempt group counseling only if qualified and if one's peer group approves of the method; (2) seek the help of another qualified person if the group is large; and (3) take safeguards when a student becomes disturbed during a group session" (pp. 40-41).

Because laws and court cases dealing with counseling malpractice are limited, this discussion includes some court cases concerning educators, physicians, and psychotherapists that have implications for counselors and others in the helping professions. Counselors, like physicians, are expected to behave according to the standards of their profession. "The law imposes on a physician who undertakes the care of a patient the obligation of due care, the exercise of an amount of skill common to his profession, without which he should not have taken the case, and a degree of care commensurate with his position." (61 Am. Jur. 2d 99)

Also, physicians have a duty to act in good faith and advise patients regarding the best possible treatment.

> The main obligation of the physician imposed upon him by law is the exercise of due care and skill in the treatment of his patient. The physician's duty of due care includes among others, his obligation to fully inform the patient of his condition, to continue to provide for medical care once the patient-physician relationship has been established, to refer him to a specialist if necessary, and to obtain the patient's informed consent to the medical treatment or operation. (61 Am. Jur. 2d 167)

Similarly, counselors should refer clients to another professional when the counselor can no longer meet the professional needs of that client. Section B-10 of *Ethical Standards* (1981) states: "If the member determines an inability to be of professional assistance to the client, the member must either avoid initiating the counseling relationship or immediately terminate that relationship. In either event, the member must suggest appropriate alternatives" (p. 2).

The following California case illustrates a malpractice litigation in education. *Peter W. v. San Francisco Unified School District* (1976), often cited in the literature as the *Peter Doe* case (Piele, 1977, 79), called attention to malpractice litigation in education (p. 80). The plaintiff charged that he had been "deprived of basic academic skills" based on two reasons. One, he maintained that the school had been negligent in providing "adequate instruction, *guidance, counseling* and/or supervision" (*Peter W. v. San Francisco Unified School District,* 1976, 856). Two, he maintained that the school "fraudulently represented" his performance to his mother (p. 862). The plaintiff lost and the Appellate Court upheld the lower court decision. The court determined that literacy is based on a "host of factors . . . beyond the control of its ministers" (p. 861). Even though the plaintiff lost, the case demonstrates to school counselors and others in the educational setting that litigation can occur and that guidance and counseling can be a legal issue in terms of meeting the educational goals of clients/students. This case has fewer implications for professional counselors or psychologists in private practice, but it certainly raises questions for school counselors. Can students bring legal charges for guidance programs that fail to provide them with adequate employment and career skills? The court decision suggests that broad skill areas such as "literacy" are difficult to prove and are affected by many factors beyond the control of educators. Yet, to school counselors it illustrates a malpractice case involving the quality of education and counseling.

Another negligence case illustrates specific charges brought against a counselor in a college setting for professional conduct. In *Bogust v. Iverson* (1960), the parents of a student brought charges against the college counselor for three counts of negligence. The parents claimed the counselor failed to get psychiatric assistance for their daughter. They also charged that the counselor did not notify them of their daughter's condition; and they claimed the counselor failed to "provide proper student guidance" (*Bogust,* 1960, 229). The counselor's duties at the college included the "maintenance of a counseling and testing center" (p. 229). The counselor saw the student professionally for approximately five months, terminated the relationship, and six weeks later, Jeannie Bogust committed suicide. In ruling for the counselor, the court stated that the counselor was a professor with a Ph.D. degree, was not trained in psychiatry or medicine, and could not be liable for a standard of conduct beyond his training and knowledge. The court concluded: "But there is no allegation of fact that would have appraised the defendant, as a reasonably prudent man, that she had such tendencies" (*Bogust,* 1960, 230). Even assuming he had secured psychiatric treatment for Jeannie or that he had advised her parents of her emotional condition or that he had not suggested termination of the interviews—it would require speculation for a jury to conclude that under such circumstances she would not have taken her life" (p. 233).

In discussing the *Bogust* case, Burgum and Anderson (1975) concluded, "The parents would have to show that a person with the background and training of the average counselor 'should have known' that Jeanie was going to commit suicide before he could be held liable" (p. 31). However, they believed that counselors today would probably not "get off this easily" (p. 31). Van Hoose and Kottler (1978) reached a similar conclusion. They explained, "A failure to take some direct precautions with a potential suicide would almost certainly be ruled negligent in today's legal climate" (pp. 99-100). Although the court found for the counselor in *Bogust,* Talbutt and Hummel (1982) stated, "The case is a reminder to counselors that litigation for negligence has been brought against a counselor with professional conduct an issue" (p. 7).

Tarasoff v. Regents of The University of California (1974), discussed in chapter 2 in terms of ethical responsibilities, should be discussed in this chapter regarding the liability issue. The 1974 court case illustrates that a physician or psychotherapist can be liable for failure to warn a victim about potential harm or danger. During a counseling session, Poddar, a patient of the college psychotherapist at the University of California at Berkeley, informed the psychotherapist that he intended to kill Tatiana Tarasoff. The psychotherapist notified the university police who detained Poddar for a short time but released him.

Poddar then proceeded to kill Tarasoff. Her parents sued the university regents, the psychotherapist, and campus police. The lower court ruled for the defendants, but the Supreme Court of California determined that the defendants were negligent in their "duty to warn" (*Tarasoff,* 1974, 565). The court explained, "We conclude that a doctor or a psychotherapist treating a mentally ill patient just as a doctor treating physical illness, bears a duty to use reasonable care to give threatened persons such warnings as are essential to avert foreseeable danger arising from his patient's condition or treatment" (p. 559).

The court also discussed public policy on privileged communication when it conflicts with necessary disclosure. "We conclude that the public policy favoring protection of the confidential character of patient-psychotherapist communications must yield in instances in which disclosure is essential to avert danger to others" (*Tarasoff,* 1974, 561). What was clear in *Tarasoff* is that the physician or psychotherapist must warn the person in danger—warning the campus police was not sufficient. The threatened person or persons in danger must be notified so they can take action to protect themselves.

Slimak and Berkowitz (1983) believe that the *Tarasoff* doctrine sets a precedent and is significant for other court rulings. They cite *Mavroudis v. Superior Court* (1980) as an example of a case that expands the *Tarasoff* doctrine. In that case Slimak and Berkowitz report that a client who was receiving psychiatric treatment attacked his parents, causing them multiple injuries. However, the client never named his parents as intended victims. The court stated the "victim(s) need not be named by the client for the therapist to break confidentiality. The therapist need only to have reasonably determined that the victim or victims were readily identifiable" (*Mavroudis,* 1980, 293).

McIntosh v. Milano (1979), a New Jersey case, illustrates a situation similar to *Tarasoff.* Lee Morgenstein, an adolescent boy referred by a school counselor, told his therapist (Milano) he had fantasies about having sex with Kimberly (a girl next door), he revealed that he had shot a BB gun at Kimberly's car when she left for a date, and he showed a knife to the psychiatrist. He further told the therapist he wanted to see Kimberly suffer, that he was angry when Kimberly moved out of her parents' home, and was upset when he could not get Kimberly's new address. He then killed Kimberly. The therapist talked with the client's parents about their son but never to Kimberly or her parents. The superior court of New Jersey determined, "A psychiatrist may have a duty to take whatever steps are reasonably necessary to protect an intended or potential victim" (*McIntosh,* 1979, 500). The court further cited *Tarasoff* by stating that a "practioner may have to protect the welfare of the community," which is similar to a physician warning third parties about contagious diseases (p. 512). Regarding confidentiality, the court determined that although New Jersey recognizes physician-patient privilege, "confidentiality cannot be considered absolute or decisive" (p. 512).

In *Leedy v. Hartnett* (1981), the United States district court in Pennsylvania decided that the hospital personnel did not have a duty to warn based on the facts in that case. The court cited *Tarasoff,* but determined that "those charged with the care of potentially dangerous people must be able to know to whom to give warnings" (Leedy, 1981, 1130). In this case the Leedys, beaten by a former Veterans Administration hospital patient, claimed that the hospital personnel should have warned them of the patient's tendency toward violence because the personnel knew he was planning to stay in their home. The Leedy's invited Hartnett into their home and on the evening in question went to a club "drinking" with Hartnett, who subsequently beat them. In this case the Leedys never claimed that Hartnett threatened them. The facts of the case indicated that Hartnett did not pose a greater danger to the Leedys than anyone else. Clearly, a therapist or other staff must have adequate information about a client's potential to harm certain victims in order to warn those in danger.

These court cases clearly indicate that therapists have a duty to warn victims; that the facts must be clear enough for the therapist to know the intended victims; and that there is a duty to warn even when victims are not named if their identities are clear. Although these court cases deal with therapists, counselors should assume that the same standards apply to them. Unfortunately, until a court case or series of cases apply specifically to counselors, it is unknown whether the courts will expect the same standards for counselors as for therapists.

Client-Counselor Relationships

The courts have determined in a number of cases that psychotherapists should not take advantage of the client-psychotherapist relationship. In *Zipkin v. Freeman* (1968), the court found the psychiatrist guilty of mishandling the transference phenomenon. The psychiatrist instructed the patient to move into his apartment over his office, they entered into a social relationship, and he encouraged her to invest money in his farm. The court found the psychiatrist guilty of professional negligence and awarded the client damages. The psychotherapist took advantage of the professional relationship for personal gain.

In *Doe v. Roe and Poe* (1977), a patient brought tort action against her psychiatrist for invading her privacy by publishing a book about her personal thoughts and feelings. The patient's former husband coauthored the book and was also named in the charges. In finding for the plaintiff, the Supreme Court of New York offered the following reasoning: "a physician who enters into an agreement with a patient to provide medical attention impliedly covenants to keep in confidence all disclosures made by the patient concerning the patient's physical or mental condition as well as all matters discovered by the physician in the course of examination or treatment" (p. 668). A strong implication for counseling is that professionals should not take advantage of the client relationship for personal gain.

The following case involves a tenured secondary-school counselor and a student in a public school setting. In *Goldin v. Board of Education* (1975), a New York appellate court determined that the school board could investigate the counselor's relationship with a female student and that the investigation was not an invasion of the counselor's privacy. The counselor was charged with sleeping with an 18-year-old student in her parents' home while they were absent. The student was a recent graduate who had received counseling from Goldin two months earlier. The court drew the following conclusion:

> A professional teacher entrusted with forming the moral and social values of our young people must accept the reality that he is held to a high or strict standard of conduct . . . approximately two months after having a particular student under his guidance, plaintiff is accused of going to bed with her. Such conduct might be susceptible to the presumption that the intimate relationship did not develop overnight.

The incident conceivably could so upset the community as to undermine the confidence of students and parents of students who now seek plaintiff's guidance. This, in turn, could go to the heart of plaintiff's ability to carry out his duties. (*Goldin*, 1975, 869-870)

A 1976 court case illustrates litigation regarding sexual abuse by a therapist. In *Roy v. Hartogs* (1976), a patient charged her psychiatrist with malpractice and was awarded $25,000 in damages. Allegedly Dr. Renatus Hartogs had sexual intercourse with his client over a period of 13 months as part of her prescribed therapy for which he charged the client. Upon ruling for the plaintiff, Judge Markowitz wrote, "While cultists expound theories of the beneficial effects of sexual psychotherapy, the fact remains that all eminent experts . . . including the American Psychiatric Association, abjure sexual contact between patient and therapist as harmful" (*Roy*, 1976, 590). This court ruling and reference to the American Psychiatric Association by the presiding justice, illustrates the importance of following one's professional code. Failure to follow "acceptable standards of treatment of the mentally disturbed" can lead to malpractice (*Roy*, 1976, 590).

Conclusion

This section identifies several areas in which counselors, psychologists, and psychotherapists might face civil liability litigation for common tort action. These areas include falling below conduct appropriate to one's profession, failing to warn or take action when someone is in danger, taking advantage of the counseling relationship for personal gain, and advising beyond one's skill and training. If counselors face malpractice charges, they would likely be judged according to the standards appropriate for the counseling profession. Consequently, counselors should be familiar with and follow their professional ethics and laws, and keep up with current litigation affecting counseling.

There are several clues that strongly suggest that counselors may face more litigation in the future. For example, the American Personnel and Guidance Association encourages members to carry liability insurance. Also, counselors function in a variety of work settings that introduce a range of problems that can lead to potential liability charges. Swanson (1980) wrote, "as credentialing of counselors increases, higher standards of care, ethical conduct and professional service will be demanded. With higher standards come greater risks of incurring civil liability" (p. 19). Thus, he also recommended that counselors carry professional liability insurance. Professional associations may offer it; for example, the American Personnel and Guidance Association (APGA) offers liability insurance for members.

CONSTITUTIONAL TORTS

Constitutional tort litigation has been increasing in recent years. Individuals are alleging violations of their constitutional and civil rights. The judicial foundation of a large number of these suits is the Civil Rights Act of 1871 codified as title 42 of the United States Code, section 1983. If an official violates the statutory or constitutional rights of another person, the official may be held personally liable for actual damages.

The statute was enacted in 1871 during the Reconstruction era, and was commonly referred to as the Ku Klux act. At that time blacks in the South were being deprived of constitutional rights by government officials. On March 23, 1871, President Grant sent a message to Congress stating that a condition of affairs existed in some states of the Union rendering life and property insecure and that the power to correct these evils was beyond control of the state authorities. Therefore, Grant urgently recommended legislation that, in the judgment of Congress, would effectually secure life, liberty and property, and the enforcement of law in all parts of the United States (cited in *Monell,* 1978, 2024). Congress responded to this message by passing the 1871 Civil Rights Act, which states:

> Every person who, under color of any statute, ordinance, regulation, custom, or usage, of any State or Territory, subjects, or causes to be subjected, any citizen of the United States or other person within the jurisdiction thereof to the deprivation of any rights, privileges or immunities secured by the Constitution and laws, shall be liable to the party injured in an action at law, suit in equity, or other proper proceeding for redress. (Title 42, United States Code, sec. 1983)

This statute was dormant for a number of years, but became the focus of litigation in the 1960s during the civil rights movement. Because the court had not established precedents for this type of litigation, each case has brought about a more definitive judicial picture of exactly the extent and meaning of the legislation.

One of the first questions to be raised was the interpretation of the word *person.* Did *person* mean just the individual, just the institution, or the individual and the institution? Plaintiffs wanted the word to be interpreted as meaning the institution rather than just the individual, because the institution would have greater fiscal resources with which to pay damages. In *Monroe v. Pape* (1961) the Supreme Court determined policemen were personally liable as individuals, but the city of Chicago was not a person and therefore was not liable. In *Monell v. New York City Department of Social Services* (1978) the Supreme Court overturned *Monroe* and declared the word *person* meant local government or institutions, such as social service agencies, school boards, town counsels, and universities. Also, local governments or institutions are not entitled to absolute immunity under this legislation. These decisions mean that a local official or employee may be sued for violating the statutory or constitutional rights of an individual; and at the same time, the local agency may also be sued as a corporate body. Therefore, those cases clearly established that the individual and the institution may be held personally liable.

Who has immunity from suit under this statute, and what is the extent of that immunity? Does the individual being sued have absolute immunity because what he or she doing is for the good of the general public (e.g., legislators)? Or does he or she have qualified immunity, which is much more limited in scope? The Supreme Court, in a series of cases, determined that absolute immunity was available as a defense for prosecutors in initiating and presenting the State's case (*Imbler v. Pachtman,* 1976) and for state legislators (*Tenny v. Brandhove,* 1951).

Prosecutors and legislators have absolute immunity; therefore, it would appear that all other state officials have qualified or conditional immunity. Qualified or conditional immunity from civil liability means an individual would not be liable as long as they are acting clearly within the scope of their authority for the betterment of those they serve. If they venture outside the scope of their authority and in doing so violate someone's rights, then they may be personally liable. One of the leading cases in establishing the extent of qualified immunity was *Scheuer v. Rhodes* (1974), where the governor of Ohio and other officials were sued after four students were shot and killed at Kent State University. The Supreme Court declared the governor of Ohio and other executive officers had qualified good-faith immunity for discretionary acts performed in the course of official conduct. Qualified immunity has been established by Supreme Court decision for superintendents of state hospitals (*O'Conner v. Donaldson,* 1975) and local school board members (*Wood v. Strickland,* 1975).

Although *individuals* may assert good faith as a defense in a constitutional tort action, a municipality has no immunity and may not assert a good faith defense (*Owen v. City of Independence,* 1980).

Any action brought under title 42 of the United States Code, section 1983, may allow an individual—be he or she a teacher, guidance counselor, student, policeman, social worker, or city manager—to collect actual damages. Generally, only actual damages will be allowed and not punitive damages. The Supreme Court "has indicated that punitive damages might be awarded in appropriate circumstances in order to punish violations of constitutional rights, *Carey v. Piphus,* (435 U.S. 247, 257, n. 11, 1978), but it never has suggested that punishment is as prominent a purpose under the statute as are compensation and deterrance" (*City of Newport v. Facts Concert, Inc.,* 1981).

It is important for public employees and governing bodies to recognize the statutory and constitutional rights of students, teachers, counselors, administrators, and custodians. Litigation in this area has covered a wide spectrum from the student to the employee. The types of actions include students and employees not being given due process, policemen being illegally dismissed, and a city being sued by a rock group for alleged civil rights violations. Therefore, it is extremely important for all individuals for their own protection and the protection of the organization to be cognizant of the rights of other individuals. The Supreme Court in *Wood v. Strickland* (1975) has said that individuals should reasonably know which actions might be the deprivation of constitutional rights.

Cases

In *Roman v. Appleby* (1983), a student and his parents brought a civil rights (42 U.S.C. sec. 1983) action against a school counselor and a social worker. The plaintiff, Alexander Roman, a tenth grade student, voluntarily went to see counselor Appleby for an interview. Eight more interviews followed, all encouraged by the counselor. The mother of the plaintiff called the counselor and acknowledged that her son was involved in counseling sessions. The parents, although knowing about the sessions, did not authorize the counselor to induce responses from the child about "his immediate family, including his affection or nonaffection or intimate relations for its members; the manner in which his parents had raised him; sex, masturbation, homosexuality, and the 'Oedipus complex'; or God, religion, heaven, hell and sin" (*Roman,* 1983, 453). During the counseling sessions, Appleby told Alexander that his parents were too strict; their religious views were too rigid and conservative; he could not function in reality; he was possibly psychotic; and that his fears of being a homosexual were normal for his age.

The counselor then arranged a conference with the parents, where the counselor gave her opinions to the parents. The counselor recommended professional help, specifically, Crisis Intervention, a mental-health counseling service. When the parents did not contact the service, the counselor referred the matter to the Chester County Children's Service (CCCS) and recommended that the student undergo psychiatric counseling. Hendry, the social worker, contacted the parents during the investigation. After the investigation, the social worker petitioned the County court to have the student adjudicated a "dependent" of the court. The petition also sought an order directing psychological and psychiatric evaluation and testing. Hendry wrote a report classifying the student as mentally unstable and emotionally disturbed, in need of psychiatric evaluation and possible treatment. This report was delivered to the student's personal physician and read by other employees of CCCS.

The parents' suit alleged a multitude of violations, including freedom of religion, because the counselor talked to the student about religion and violation of privacy rights.

The United States Federal District Court found that the counselor and social worker had a defense of qualified or "good faith" immunity. "The immunity concept is based upon the need to insure principled and conscientious governmental decision-making" (*Roman,* 1983, 455). The court determined the appropriate judicial test would be "that good faith immunity will defeat a claim so long as the official conduct does not violate 'clearly established statutory or constitutional rights' of which a reasonable person would have known" (p. 455). The student did not have any clearly established rights violated.

The court noted that the constitutional rights of children, parents, administrators, and teachers are all competing in the schools. But these rights are not absolute, and must be balanced against the rights of other individuals and also the rights of the state.

> Courts have stated repeatedly that where a child's emotional well-being may be threatened, or where there is a potential for significant social burdens, the state's interest in his mental health will override free exercise claims . . . .
>
> Given the competing constitutional claims, which are inherently involved in a public school setting, including a guidance counselor's first amendment right of free speech, it cannot be said that Appleby's conduct violated plaintiff's clearly established constitutional right to freely exercise their religion or with their right to maintain a private family relationship without unnecessary governmental interference. The mere fact that Appleby and Alexander discussed potentially sensitive topics did not give rise to a constitutional level. There is no allegation that Alexander was compelled to attend the counseling sessions nor threatened with discipline or removal from school if he failed to cooperate. (*Roman,* 1983, 456-457)

A 15-year-old girl, Valerie Dick, had conversations with Maureen McCarthy, a guidance counselor, as part of group discussions at St. James High School. Later, while talking privately with the counselor, Valerie expressed a desire to leave her home because of frequent family arguments. The student then raised the subject of foster care. Later that day the counselor telephoned a mental health worker, Deborah Hunter, to ask whether Valerie would be eligible for foster care. Hunter told the counselor there appeared to be insufficient grounds, but she would check. After an investigation of the family, Hunter and other Watonwan County Welfare Department officials met with Valerie; and subsequently her parents were arrested and confined in a detoxification center for one weekend on a petition signed by welfare department officials. They were released on the stipulation they attend alcohol counseling sessions. The parents then filed suit against welfare officials, the sheriff, county attorney, and the school guidance counselor for allegedly violating their civil rights under the United States Code (title 42, sec. 1983).

In deciding whether the counselor had violated the parents civil rights, the Minnesota District Court found no evidence that the counselor sought to have the parents committed. The court said:

> Other considerations weigh against holding McCarthy liable under section 1983. As an official engaged in social services and charged with child care, McCarthy had a duty under Minnesota law to report the suspected neglect or abuse of Valerie (statute ommitted). In addition, McCarthy is entitled to good faith immunity under federal law. The plaintiffs have provided no evidence, other than the unsupported allegations of counsel, that McCarthy did not act in good faith. The plaintiffs cannot rely on "bare allegations of malice" to defeat the granting of summary judgment. In the absence of any evidence of a malicious motive on McCarthy's part, the Court must grant her motion for summary judgment on the plaintiff's section 1983 claim. (*Dick v. Watonwan County,* 1982, 996)

CHAPTER GUIDELINES

1. Counselors may face malpractice litigation when their behavior falls below standards of conduct appropriate for their profession or when they go beyond their skill and training.
2. Counselors are expected to act according to standards appropriate for their profession. They have a duty to act in good faith and advise clients regarding the best treatment.
3. Counselors should warn or take appropriate action when the client or others are in danger.
4. Counselors who follow professional standards of conduct are most likely to meet the court's definition of good faith and appropriate conduct.
5. Laws and court cases dealing specifically with counseling and malpractice are limited; thus, implications must be drawn from court cases and laws pertaining to physicians, psychotherapists, and other similar professionals.
6. Court cases cited in this chapter illustrate some negligence charges brought against psychotherapists and educators. The cases serve as examples to professionals that negligence charges may occur both in the educational and private setting.
7. Counselors should not take advantage of clients for personal gains.

Cases cited in this chapter illustrate malpractice litigation for sexual and financial abuse.

8. There are several clues that suggest that counselors may face more litigation in the future. For example, American Personnel and Guidance Association members are encouraged to carry liability insurance.

SITUATIONAL DISCUSSIONS

Situation 1: Identify some potential danger areas that might lead to civil liability for counselors.

Situation 2: For what purposes do professional standards exist? Can these guidelines aid counselors in litigation? If so, how?

Situation 3: Give two illustrations (one positive and one negative) of professional counselors advising beyond their professional training and skill.

Situation 4: Do you believe that people in the helping profession will face more litigation in the future? Why?

Situation 5: Identify some situations from your work setting that would require you to make referrals to other professionals rather than work with the client yourself.

REFERENCES

Alexander, D., 1976, Legal issues in guidance, in *School Guidance Services,* T. H. Hohenshil and J. H. Miles, eds., Kendall/Hunt, Dubuque, Iowa, pp. 219-246.

Alexander, K., R. Corns, and W. McCann, 1969, *Public School Law,* West, St. Paul, Minn.

Burgum, T., and S. Anderson, 1975, *The Counselor and the Law,* APGA Press, Washington, D.C.

Ethical Standards of the American Personnel and Guidance Association, 1981, Washington, D.C.

Piele, P. K., ed., 1977, *The Yearbook of School Law,* NOLPE, Topeka, Kansas.

Slimak, R. E., and S. F. Berkowitz, 1983, The university and college counselor center and malpractice suits, *Personnel and Guidance Journal* **61:**291-295.

Swanson, C. D., 1980, Professional credentialing and regulation, *Virginia Personnel and Guidance Journal* **8:**15-19.

Talbutt, L., and D. Hummel, 1982, Legal and ethical issues impacting on counselors, *Counseling and Human Development* **14**(6):1-12.

Van Hoose, W. H., and T. Kottler, 1978, *Ethical and Legal Issues in Counseling and Psychotherapy,* Jossey-Bass, San Francisco.

LEGAL REFERENCES

61 American Jurisprudence 2d 99 (1981).
Bogust v. Iverson, 102 N.W.2d 228 (S.C. Wis. 1960).
Carey v. Piphus, 435 U.S. 247 (1978).
Dick v. Watonwan, 551 F. Supp. 983 (D.C. Minn. 1982).
Doe v. Roe and Poe, 400 N.Y.S.2d 668 (S.C. N.Y. 1977).
Goldin v. Board of Education, 357 N.Y.S.2d 867 (1975).
Guerrieri v. Tyson, 24 A.2d 248 (Sup. C. Pa. 1942).
Imbler v. Pachtman, 424 U.S. 409 (1976).
Johnston v. Rodis, 251 F.2d 917 (D.C. Cir. 1958).
Leedy v. Hartnett, 510 F. Supp. 1125 (M.D. Pa. 1981).
McIntosh v. Milano, 403 A.2d 500 (Sup. C. N.J. 1979).
Monell v. New York City Department of Social Services, 436 U.S. 658 (1978).
Monroe v. Pape, 365 U.S. 167 (1961).
City of Newport v. Facts Concert, Inc., 453 U.S. 247 (1981).
O'Connor v. Donaldson, 422 U.S. 563 (1975).
Owen v. City of Independence, 445 U.S. 622 (1980).
Peter W. v. San Francisco Unified School District, 131 Cal. Rptr. 854 (Calif. Cir. 1976).
Roman v. Appleby, 558 F. Supp. 449 (E.D. Pa. 1983).
Roy v. Hartogs, 381 N.Y.S. 2d 587 (S.C. N.Y. 1976).
Scheuer v. Rhodes, 416 U.S. 232 (1974).
Tarasoff v. Regents of University of California, 529 P.2d 553 (S.C. Calif. 1974).
Tenny v. Brandhove, 341 U.S. 367 (1951).
Title 20 United States Code, 1232g, P.L. 93 380 (1974).
Title 42 United States Code, § 1983 (1871).
Wood v. Strickland, 420 U.S. 308 95 S.C. 992 (1975).
Zipkin v. Freeman, 436 S.W.2d 753 (S.C. Mo. 1968).

Chapter 6

Libel and Slander

To guard against litigation for libel and slander, counselors should be familiar with issues regarding this area and should follow professional guidelines for avoiding legal pitfalls. The American Personnel and Guidance Associations (APGA) *Ethical Standards* (1981), "Ethical Principles of Psychologists" (1981), and the American School Counselor Association's (ASCA) "Position Statements" (1983) provide such guidelines. This chapter addresses some key issues related to libel and slander and offers practical recommendations for counselors.

Both libel and slander refer to the defamation of a person's character or reputation. Historically libel has meant defamation expressed in written form, whereas slander is expressed by word of mouth. Alexander, Corns, and McCann (1969) offered the following definition and explanation:

> Slander and libel consist of false and intentionally published or communicated statements . . . If the statement is communicated by word of mouth or gestures, it is known as slander. If it is communicated in writing, printing, or pictures, it is libel. Simply stated, libel is written defamation and slander is oral defamation. (P. 325)

Selected portions of this chapter are used with permission from L. C. Talbutt, 1983, Libel and Slander: A potential problem for the 1980's *The School Counselor* **30:**164-168.

The necessary elements for a tort of libel and slander are: "(1) a false statement concerning another was published or communicated; (2) the statement brought hatred, disgrace, ridicule or contempt on another person; (3) damages resulted from the statement" (Alexander, Corns, and McCann, 1969, 325). Educators, including counselors, would be likely to face litigation for libel and slander if these three factors were present unless the statements were true or privileged. Both of these defenses are discussed in this chapter.

Breezer (1981, 577) gave three reasons for litigation for defamation. First, it is "vindication of a person's good name." Second, an individual can get compensation for damage due to false statements. Third, "punishing an offender can serve as a warning to others."

IMPLICATIONS FOR COUNSELORS

Bergum and Anderson (1975) noted that there are few court cases involving libel and slander in education; however, they reminded school counselors that they have "no more right to defame a student than any member of society has a right to defame any other member" (p.71). Since 1975, several cases involving education have occurred. Libel and slander, then, are likely areas of litigation for counselors. Killian (1970) identified three examples that illustrate risks for school counselors: "(a) talking on the telephone about a child's mental test score; (b) telling a bystander in the office about a boy's failing grade; and (c) relaying information about a student to a third party when it is clearly not a professional obligation" (p. 423).

Hummel and Talbutt wrote, "More than at any time in the history of counseling, counselors must know their legal boundaries and responsibilities" (1980, 2). Counselors, because of the nature of their work, have many opportunities for defamation that could result in litigation. They are privy to conversations, records, and personal information and they communicate with a range of individuals who may pressure them to reveal confidential information.

Although counselors and psychologists in private practice are subject to litigation for libel and slander, those who work for organizations, especially public schools, face unique pressures that could lead to libel and slander.

Ladd (1971) gave three reasons why conflict exists when a counselor works for both a client and an organization. First, Ladd explained the "counselor's loyalty is divided" (p. 262). The counselor may become interested in "protecting and enhancing the organization . . . and may allow this interest to interfere with his dedication to serving his client" (p. 262). Second, others in the organization "may pressure a counselor to do things differently . . . ." (p. 262). Third, the size of an organization leads to a greater collection and storage of information than a professional counselor working alone.

Patterson (1971) noted that "the school counselor is in the most difficult situation" (p. 255). He identified two problems unique to the school setting (p. 256-257). First, teachers and administrators pressure counselors into disclosing confidential information. Teachers refer students for counseling and desire feedback from counselors. Patterson concluded that even "counselors who subscribe to the principle of confidentiality often depart from its practice under pressure" (1971, 256). In commenting on the relationship between counselors and teachers, Aubrey (1973) agreed with Patterson. Aubrey maintained that counselors must "persuade teachers to release students [from class] for guidance purposes" (p. 347). The second problem that Patterson identified in the school setting is that the clients are minors. The author stated:

> The school counselor is vulnerable to requests and pressures from parents. Although the legal rights of parents to inspect records does not extend to inspection of the counselor's mind, parental pressures on counselors for information regarding their children are not uncommon. (P. 258)

COURT CASES AND DISCUSSION

Several historical court cases have implications for counselors in the area of libel and slander. In *Baskett v. Crossfield* (1921), a college president was charged with libel because of two letters he wrote to the father of a student. The letters explained that Baskett has been asked to withdraw from college for indecently exposing himself from the window of his dormitory room. In ruling in favor of the president, the Kentucky circuit court reasoned that he was acting *in loco parentis* and it reached the following conclusion:

> In the performance of this duty the president of the university had the right to act, write, and say of and concerning the dismissed student what a reasonably prudent and considerate official of a college would under like circumstances have done and said. (*Baskett*, 1921, 675-676)

Baskett concluded that the letters written by the college president were made in good faith. Also, the court pointed out that the burden was on the plaintiff to show malice.

In *Kenny v. Gurley* (1923), action was brought on behalf of a student against the school principal, medical director, and dean of women for libelous letters written to the parents. Action was based on statements pertaining to the student's having a venereal disease and "not living right." The Alabama Supreme Court concluded that no malice existed and reversed the lower court ruling, which had awarded the plaintiff damages against the medical director and dean of women. In addressing the matter of conditionally privileged communication, the court explained:

When words are conditionally privileged, "the law simply withdraws the legal inference of malice, or express malice, or malice in fact, is not shown", the burden of proof being, as stated, upon the plaintiff in respect of the establishment of the presence of such malice. (*Kenny,* 1923, 37)

Also, the court pointed out that "the use of intemperate language" did not void the communication privilege (p. 37). In addition, the court reasoned that proving a statement untrue did not necessarily mean that malice existed. "The fact that the statement is admitted or proved to be untrue is no evidence that it was made maliciously, through proof that defendant knew it was untrue when he made it would be evidence of malice" (p. 37).

In a more recent U.S. Supreme Court ruling, *Hutchinson v. Proxmire* (1979) determined that a U.S. senator did not have absolute immunity from defamatory statements in press releases and newsletters. Rather, absolute immunity was limited to action in the Senate. For example, a speech in the Senate would be wholly immune from liability, but newsletters and press releases—not part of the deliberative process—were not immune. In this case immunity applied only to official duties, and then only those specified as essential to the Senate.

In *Iverson v. Frandsen* (1956), libel charges were placed against a psychologist for language used in a psychological report. The report stated that the plaintiff's "intelligence quotient . . . classified her as 'feeble-minded', at a high grade moron level." (pp. 899-900). The Utah circuit court court reasoned that the report "though qualifiedly privileged, was positively free from any actionable malice whatsoever" (p. 900). The court pointed out that the psychologist followed standard procedures and that the report "was as accurate" as could have been made and concluded, "It was a professional report made by a public servant in good faith, representing his best judgment, and therefore could not be maliciously false" (p. 900).

Two court cases dealing with public school officials illustrate the courts' decision on slander. In *Stanley v. Taylor* (1972), action was taken by a school principal against a teacher for slander. In this case the teacher became angry at the principal and stated:

I would like to know what this school system is coming to, anyway, you are the poorest excuse for a principal I have ever seen in my life. You sit there all day long and write excuse after excuse . . . you are plain stupid . . . you are a disgrace to the profession. (P. 825)

Then the teacher stated,"[Y]ou are just like that old Lee Harvey Oswald that shot and killed President Kennedy, and that old Jack Ruby" (826).

The Fourth District Appellate Court of Illinois determined that the teacher's statements were spontaneous, were made in the hearing distance of only a few persons, and did not damage the principal's reputation. The court explained that defamation is not based on the plaintiff's feelings but damage to reputation in the eyes of others. In fact, the court found that the teacher's action reflected more adversely on the teacher than the principal.

In a similar case, *McGowen v. Prentice* (1977), the Louisiana Fourth District Court determined that the principal did not defame a teacher in the school. The principal made the statement to a teacher concerning another faculty member, "[S]he was a strange bird . . . . she did things in a strange way." (p. 57). Then when the teacher present defended the second teacher, the principal stated, "[T]hats why you understand her so well, because you are both nuts" (p. 56). The teacher to whom the principal was talking sued the principal for damages. The court determined that casual remarks made in informal conversation do not constitute defamation.

Although neither of the two previously discussed public school cases resulted in defamation, they illustrate that slander charges can result in today's legal climate. Counselors, educators, psychologists, and others should avoid defamatory statements to clients and other professionals. Such statements could lead to charges of slander and defamation if the comments damage an individual's reputation.

DEFENSES FOR LIBEL AND SLANDER

In addition to understanding the danger for legal problems regarding libel and slander, counselors must also understand the two common defenses for defamation—truth and privileged communication. The historical Kentucky Circuit Court decision in *Baskett v. Crossfield* (1921) identified these two defenses. Truth is a defense unless the statements are malicious. Counselors should obviously act in good faith and be truthful. Ware (1971) concluded that counselors who follow ethical standards would probably meet the legal standards of good faith.

Baskett cited several points of law regarding "truth and privileged communication" as defenses for defamation:

> In an action of libel, the truth is always a complete defense, although the publication may be inspired by malice or an ill will and be libelous per se. . . . If a communication comes within the class denominated absolute privileged or qualifiedly privileged, no recovery can be had. (1921, 675)

Baskett also gave the following explanations for qualified privileged communication:

> (1) That the communication was made by the defendant in good faith, without malice, not voluntarily, but in answer to an inquiry, and in the reasonable protection of his own interest or performance of a duty to society; (2) that the defendant must honestly believe the communication to be true; (3) there must have been reasonable

or probable grounds known to him for the suspicion; (4) that the communication, if made in answer to an inquiry, must not go further than to truly state the facts upon which the suspicion was grounded, and to satisfy the inquirer that there were reasons for the suspicion . . . (7) A qualifiedly privileged communication takes place when the circumstances are held to preclude any presumptions of malice, but still leave the party responsible for both falsehood and malice if affirmatively shown. (8) Where a party makes a communication and such a communication is prompted by a duty owed either to the public or to a third party, or the communication is one in which the party has an interest, the communication is privileged if made in good faith and without actual malice. (P. 675)

Iverson also cited the legal definitions for absolute privileged communication and conditional privileged communication as they relate to libel and slander.

Absolutely privileged statements or communications are confined to very narrow fields, such as judicial proceedings, statements of executive officers made in the discharge of their duties, and legislative proceedings. Conditionally privileged communications, when made in good faith, without malice, to a person having a corresponding interest or duty, are nonactionable. (1956, 898)

Numerous court cases illustrate the court's thinking on conditional privileged communication as a defense in libel and slander cases. In *Hett v. Ploetz* (1963), a speech therapist sued for defamation owing to a letter of recommendation written by the school's superintendent to a prospective employer. The Wisconsin state supreme court ruled that the superintendent, whose name had been given as a reference, was privileged to give a critical appraisal of a former employee. Also, the superintendent's letter did not exceed the scope of the inquiry.

In *Green v. Kinsella* (1971), a guidance counselor claimed that a performance evaluation communicated to administrators by school board employees contained "false, scandalous, and defamatory statements" (p. 782). The New York state supreme court dismissed the complaint and stated that the plaintiff would have to prove malice or actual ill will. Also, the court determined that the communications were matters in which school board employees had an interest, and the communication was to persons with similar interests or duties. Thus, defendants were protected by qualified privilege.

The New York state supreme court case, *Konowitz v. Archway School Inc.* (1978) illustrates a ruling in which the teacher was granted a trial. In that case, the teacher was employed for several months, received a letter from the curriculum director describing her as capable and cooperative and alleging that she was discharged for budgetary reasons. However, when the Teachers'

Registry requested the reason for the teacher's dismissal, the school gave the impression that the teacher was dismissed because she was ineffective. The court ruled that the discrepancy between the alleged libelous statement and the reason given plaintiff for dismissal was sufficient to raise a question of malice.

Although none of the cases cited deal with counselors per se, counselors work in situations open to the potential for libel and slander. They write recommendations to employers and institutions of higher education, release records, and consult with families and interested parties concerning clients. Access to information and pressures to release it place counselors in a vulnerable position.

Counselors should also note that libel and slander are serious charges and that ethically those in the helping professions should not bring harm to another by false statements or ridicule. It is possible that counselors could err regarding libel and slander owing to lack of knowledge about potential danger areas. Speaking about a client in front of a third party, revealing client information without authorization or to unauthorized individuals, revealing more information than requested, defaming another in front of others, and speaking or writing falsely about another could lead to libel and slander charges when these actions bring hurt to, or damage, another.

As the previous court cases have suggested, counselors should be truthful and report only data they believe is true. Counselors should report student behavior objectively and factually and should avoid jargon that can be misinterpreted. Butler, Moran, and Vanderpool (1974) warned counselors that "anecdotal reports should be stripped to the bare facts and devoid of value judgments" (p. 42). Communications should be made in answer to a request and made only when such a duty exists. Counselors should believe the communication to be true and should not go beyond the necessary facts. Also, counselors are reminded against communicating in the presence of uninvolved parties. Ware (1971) offered the following advice to counselors:

> Communications made to third persons in good faith on any subject matter in which the person communicating has an interest, or in reference to which he has a duty, is qualifiedly privileged if the communications are made to a person having a corresponding interest or duty whether the duty is legal or only social or moral. (P. 308)

Ware also explained two limitations of the privileged relationship rule. First, communications should not be made in front of others who do not possess a similar interest or duty. Second, the privilege is stronger if the communication is made at the request of another. For example, a school counselor could report to a school principal or other school officials and be covered by the privileged communication rule; but the counselor could not malign a student in front of other students, the public, or other professionals not involved with the student (Ware, 1971).

RECOMMENDATIONS FOR COUNSELORS

Counselors should remember their professional guidelines and keep in mind the implications of the court cases cited. Besides *Ethical Standards* (1981) of the American Personnel and Guidance Association (APGA), which address confidentiality, in 1983 the American School Counselor Association (ASCA) presented a position statement on student records that addressed many of the issues identified in this chapter. The following guidelines can help counselors avoid legal problems related to libel and slander.

1. Counselors should maintain confidentiality unless there is danger to the client or others or unless the counselor has a legal obligation to testify in a court of law. Section B-2 of *Ethical Standards* (1981) states, "The counseling relationship and information resulting therefrom be kept confidential, consistent with the obligations of the member as a professional person." Section B-4, on the counseling relationship, states, "When the client's condition indicated that there is clear and imminent danger to the client or others, the member must take reasonable personal action or inform responsible authorities" (p. 2).
2. Counselors should not reveal confidential information over the telephone. Guideline 9 of the ASCA "Position Statements" (1983) explained: "Counselors must not discuss matters over the telephone. A counselor should insist that a request for information be made in writing on official stationery" (p. 287).
3. Counselors should allow only appropriate individuals access to confidential information. Guideline 5 of the ASCA "Position Statement" states: "Counselors must be concerned about individuals who have access to confidential information" (p. 6).
4. Counselors should assume responsibility for educating other staff members in the school about the privacy rights of students. Guideline 6 of the ASCA "Position Statement" states: "All faculty and administrative personnel should receive in-service training concerning the privacy rights of students. Counselors should assume the primary responsibility for educating school personnel in this area" (p. 287).
5. Counselors should act in good faith at all times regarding confidential information about students. Such information should not be reported

to uninvolved parties or revealed in front of those professionally uninvolved. Counselors who act out of malice or display improper behavior may be subject to libel or slander damages. On privileged communication as a defense against libel or slander, guideline 2 of the ASCA "Position Statement" declared:

> Communications made in good faith concerning a student may be classified as privileged by the courts, and the communicating parties will be protected by law against legal actions seeking damages for libel and slander. Generally, it may be said that an occasion of this particular privilege arises when one acts in the bona fide discharge of a public or private duty. This privilege may be abused or lost by malice, improper and unjustifiable motive, bad faith, or excessive publication. (P. 288)

6. Psychologists are reminded about the importance of confidentiality in the "Ethical Principles of Psychologists" (1981):

> Information obtained in clinical or consulting relationships . . . is discussed only for professional purposes and only with persons clearly concerned with the case. Psychologists who present personal information obtained during the course of professional work, in writings, lectures, or other public forums either obtain adequate prior consent . . . or adequately disguise all identifying information. (P. 636)

Psychologists and counselors who follow the ethical principles cited would likely avoid libel and slander litigation resulting from improper disclosure of client information. Revealing client information to unauthorized individuals—especially when such data could damage or harm a person's character, employment opportunities, or status in the community—could lead to litigation. Revealing confidential information in a speech, lectures, or writings could lead to defamation charges.

CHAPTER GUIDELINES

Counselors, psychologists, and educators face potential litigation for libel and slander. Libel and slander refer to defamation of another's reputation. If the defamation is communicated by word of mouth, it is slander; but if it is communicated in writing, it is libel.

1. Counselors should avoid statements (written or spoken) that could damage a client's character or reputation.
2. Counselors should not misuse or misrepresent client data. Counselors who adhere to PL 93-380 (see Appendix C) would most likely follow the proper procedures for releasing client information.
3. School counselors face unique problems. Pressures from parents and other school personnel can lead to misuse of client information.

4. Counselors should follow the suggestions drawn from the previously discussed court cases and keep abreast of legal decisions as they occur regarding libel and slander.
5. Truth and privileged communication are two recognized defenses against libel and slander; thus, counselors should be truthful and act in good faith.
6. Avoiding libeling and slandering are legal obligations for all citizens. Those in the helping professions have professional and ethical responsibilities as well.

SITUATIONAL DISCUSSIONS

Situation 1: Discuss the differences between libel and slander. How does the work setting for counselors pose special problems leading to libel and slander?

Situation 2: List some professional steps that might help counselors avoid potential libel and slander problems.

Situation 3: Are there professional guidelines helpful to counselors regarding libel and slander? If so, identify.

Situation 4: Identify a hypothetical situation that could lead to libel or slander for counselors.

Situation 5: Are counselors who work for organizations or agencies in greater danger from libel and slander litigation than those who work in private practice? If so, why?

REFERENCES

Alexander, K., R. Corns, and W. McCann, 1969, *Public School Law,* West, St. Paul, Minn.

American School Counselor Association, 1983, Position statements, *School Counselor* **20:**1-8.

Aubrey, R. F., 1973, Organizational victimization of school counselors, *School Counselor* **20:**346-347.

Breezer, B., 1981, Criticism of teachers and the law of defamation: How extensive is the shield of protection? *Phi Delta Kappan* **62:**577-583.

Burgum, T., and S. Anderson, 1975, *The Counselor and the Law,* APGA Press, Washington, D.C.

Butler, H. E., Jr., K. D. Moran, and F. A. Vanderpool, 1974, Legal aspects of student records, *School Psychology Digest* **3:**31-43.

Ethical principles of psychologists, 1981, *American Psychologist* **36:**633-638.

Ethical standards of the American Personnel and Guidance Association, 1981, Washington, D.C.

Hummel, D., and L. Talbutt, 1980, Message from the guest editors, *Virginia Personnel and Guidance Journal* **8:**2.

Killian, J. D., 1970, The law, the counselor, and student records, *Personnel and Guidance Journal* **48:**423-432.

Ladd, E. F., Counselors, confidences, and the civil liberties of clients, *Personnel and Guidance Journal* **50:**261-267.

Patterson, C. H., 1971, Are ethics different in different settings? *Personnel and Guidance Journal* **50:**254-259.

Talbutt, L. C., 1983, Libel and Slander: A potential problem for the 1980's, *School Counselor* **30:**164-168.

Ware, M., 1971, The law and counselor ethics, *Personnel and Guidance Journal* **50:**305-310.

LEGAL REFERENCES

Baskett v. Crossfield, 228 S.W. 673 (Ky. Cir. 1921).

Green v. Kinsella, 319 N.Y.S.2d 780 (S.C. N.Y. 1971).

Hett v. Ploetz, 121 N.W.2d 270 (S.C. Wis. 1963).

Hutchinson v. Proxmire, 99 S. Ct. 2675 (1979).

Iverson v. Frandsen, 237 F2d (Utah Cir. 1956).

Kenny v. Gurley, 95 So. 34 (S.C. Ala. 1923).

Konowitz v. Archway School Inc., 409 N.Y.S.2d 757 (S.C. N.Y. 1978).

McGowen v. Prentice 341 So.2d 55 (La. Cir. 1977).

Stanley v. Taylor, 278 N.E.2d 824 (4th D. Ill. 1972).

Part II

WORKING WITHIN THE EDUCATIONAL SYSTEM

Chapter 7

Student Rights and Due Process

STUDENT RIGHTS

Historically, attending public schools in this country was considered a privilege. Educators acted with impunity in disciplining students in whatever manner they deemed appropriate. The courts upheld this authority, and numerous cases illustrate this control. Students were expelled for joining social fraternities, smoking in public, or going to the movies on a weekday evening in violation of a school prohibition. The legal doctrine for upholding school authority was *in loco parentis,* which means "in place of the parents." Because students were required to attend school under compulsory attendance statutes, which had been legally upheld under the police power of the state, the courts believed educators should stand in place of the parent for the welfare of the child. When the *in loco parentis* concept was combined with the belief that attending school was a privilege, school authorities were given tremendous power.

A case in 1913 stated that school

> authorities stand *in loco parentis* concerning the physical and moral welfare and mental training of the pupils, and we are unable to see why, to that end, they may not make any rule or regulation for the government or betterment of their pupils that a parent could for the same purpose. (*Gott v. Berea College,* 1913)

In some situations it appears the concept did not work entirely for the welfare of the child but to the child's detriment, because school officials controlled aspects of the student's life far beyond the school's boundaries.

After World War II, tremendous societal changes resulted in questioning certain values and customs throughout the country. One of these issues was the appropriate status of minorities in all phases of society. Perhaps the most important case ever litigated in the United States concerned the recognition that separate but equal school facilities are inherently unequal. This famous decree was handed down by the United States Supreme Court in *Brown v. Board of Education of Topeka,* (1954) declaring separate but equal facilities and programs was a violation of the equal protection clause of the Fourteenth Amendment. Because it recognized the importance of education to society, this significant decision also diminished the influence of the *in loco parentis* concept and of the privilege doctrine for students in public schools. It also helped establish a new legal doctrine. The Court in *Brown* said:

> Today, education is perhaps the most important function of state and local governments .... It is the very foundation of good citizenship. Today, it is a principal instrument in awakening the child to cultural values, in preparing him for later professional training, and in helping him to adjust normally to his environment. In these days, it is doubtful that any child may reasonably be expected to succeed in life if he is denied the opportunity of an education. Such an opportunity, where the state has undertaken to provide it, is a *right* which must be made available to all on equal terms. (Emphasis added)

During the late fifties and the beginning of the sixties, there was no clear definition of the relationship between the student and the school. Then, in 1961 in *Dixon v. Alabama,* the Fifth United States Circuit Court of Appeals determined that going to school was a property right and school officials could not summarily expel a student without granting the individual procedural due process. The court made no attempt to establish strict procedural guidelines for due process. Schools were required to afford the student minimal procedural due process, which the court termed "fundamental fairness." It was specified that "the notice should contain a statement of the specific charges and grounds which, if proven, would justify expulsion .... The nature of the hearing should vary depending upon the circumstances of the particular case" (*Dixon,* 1961, 158). Therefore, the courts for the first time established that procedural due process was required for expulsion and that students had a constitutional property right to attend school.

In 1969 the United States Supreme Court handed down the landmark decision of *Tinker v. Des Moines* (1969). The Court established that students have substantive constitutional rights. The Court said:

> School officials do not possess absolute authority over their students. Students in school as well as out of school are "persons" under our Constitution. They are possessed of *fundamental rights* which the State must respect . . . In our system, students may not be regarded as closed-circuit recipients of only that which the State chooses to communicate. They may not be confined to the expression of those sentiments that are officially approved. In the absence of a specific showing of constitutionally valid reasons to regulate their speech, students are entitled to freedom of expression of their views. (Emphasis added)

The "fundamental rights" that were referred to in the *Tinker* decision are those liberty and property rights that a public school student possesses. Therefore students do not leave their constitutional rights at the "schoolhouse gate." When *Tinker* was handed down by the Court, it, like *Dixon,* diminished again the *in loco parentis* doctrine. Although diminished and more restricted than in the past, *in loco parentis* is still a viable legal concept. However, the privilege doctrine was destroyed and a new doctrine emerged: the right doctrine. It was now recognized that students had constitutional rights that could not be ignored by school officials. The schools are required to recognize the constitutional rights of students, but these rights are not absolute. As has been said may times, we have the First Amendment right of freedom of speech; but freedom of speech does not grant the right to "falsely shout 'fire' in a crowded theater." Such an action would be dangerous and disruptive and beyond those reasonable rights established in the Constitution; therefore, there are definite limits to constitutional rights.

The Supreme Court in *Tinker* recognized the limits of student rights and set forth what is commonly called the Tinker test. The Tinker test establishes that if a student "materially or substantially" interferes with the rights of other students or the operation of the school environment, then the disruptive student may be disciplined even if expressing a protected right. Students who have disrupted the school environment by walking out of assemblies, blocking hallways, wearing racial insignias, or participating in disruptive protests have all been disciplined by the schools because this behavior "materially and substantially" disrupts and, therefore, fails the Tinker test.

By 1970 the Supreme Court had determined that students being expelled possessed both substantive constitutional rights (*Tinker*) and procedural due process rights (*Dixon v. Alabama,* 1961). There is a legal distinction between expulsion and suspension. Expulsion from school is for a long period of time or may be indefinite; also, expulsion in most states can only be sanctioned by the school board. Suspension from school is for a short period of time, and usually statutory authority to suspend is granted to the principal or a designated teacher. The due process rights of students in regard to expulsion was legally defined in the *Dixon* case and in other cases, but specific due-process procedures for suspension had not been established by the early seventies. Therefore the question was raised in numerous court cases as to whether or not procedural due process had to be given a student who was suspended for a short period of time.

In 1975 in *Goss v. Lopez,* the United States Supreme Court clarified the issue of whether short term suspension required due process. Students who were suspended for up to 10 days without any due process contended that their due process rights under the Fourteenth Amendment rights had been violated. The court observed that short term suspensions are a milder deprivation than an expulsion; but while the weight and severity of the deprivation may determine the extent of the hearing, the hearing must be provided if a basic right is involved. Going to school is a property right; and before an individual's property right may be removed, due process must be administered. Because a suspension for a short duration is not a great deprivation, then procedural due process may be informal. Fundamental fairness dictates students must have the right to tell their side of the story. Because short term suspensions require a less formal procedure, the hearing would not provide all of the features of a formal hearing. The hearing does not

> afford the student the opportunity to secure counsel, to confront and cross-examine witnesses . . . to impose even truncated trial-type procedures might well overwhelm administrative facilities in many places and, by diverting resources, cost more than it would save in educational effectiveness. Moreover, further formalizing the suspension process and escalating its formality and adversary nature may not only make it too costly as a regular disciplinary tool but also destroy its effectiveness as part of the teaching process. (*Goss,* 1975)

The Supreme Court in *Goss* established that students have a constitutional right, founded in the liberty rights of the Fourteenth Amendment, where information contained in school records is concerned. This liberty interest comes into play when the student's good name, reputation, honor, or integrity is at stake. Therefore student records containing information about suspensions, in the absence of due process to validate the charges, had to be expunged.

Students have a right to procedural due process before they are suspended or expelled. But what is due process? What process is due an individual and under what conditions?

DUE PROCESS

The concept of due process originated with the Magna Charta signed by the king of England in 1215. It acknowledged that individuals could not be imprisoned, outlawed, banished, or hurt in any way unless they were judged by their peers according to the law. Persons have certain natural rights and government-granted rights that may not be negated except by appropriate procedures established by law and as judged by their peers. This basic concept was transferred from England to the United States and may be found in the early constitutions of the New England states. This fundamental idea of not having a basic right jeopardized or removed except after a fair hearing was enunciated in the Fifth Amendment of the Bill of Rights. "[N]or shall any person . . . be deprived of life, liberty, or property without due process of law."

The Fifth Amendment applies to the federal government, meaning that the federal government can not take away life, liberty, or property without granting due process. However, could a *state* deprive an individual of life, liberty, or property without due process? The first answer was basically *yes.* Then in 1868 the Fourteenth Amendment to the United States Constitution was passed. This amendment permitted the courts to apply to the states the first ten amendments to the Constitution (the Bill of Rights). It also provides that "no state shall deprive a person of life, liberty or property without due process of law." Positively stated, this concept means that a state may deprive a citizen of life, liberty, or property but must first afford that individual due process. Because education is not mentioned in the federal Constitution, it is, therefore, left to the states through the reserved powers of the Tenth Amendment.

Student rights' cases are usually brought under the provision of the Fourteenth Amendment. This provision comes about because education is reserved to the states through the Tenth Amendment, and the Fourteenth Amendment provides that no *state* shall deprive a person of life, liberty or property without due process of law. The Tenth Amendment states: "The powers not delegated to the United States by the Constitution, nor prohibited by it to the States, are reserved to the states respectively or to the people."

Procedural Due Process

There are two types of due process. The first to be interpreted and defined by the courts was procedural due process, a prescribed procedure that must be followed before a person may be deprived of rights, particularly life, liberty, or property. The basic concept revolves around the fact that government may take away anything you have. Government may take your life through capital punishment, your house through eminent domain, your liberty by incarcerating you, your child because of neglect or child abuse, your right to go to school by expulsion or suspension from school, or anything else you may have.

The due process concept is flexible in that procedural due process becomes more formal as that which is intended to be taken away increases in value or seriousness. If an individual is going to be imprisoned—the removal of liberty—then procedural due process is very formal and guarantees the right to an attorney, trial, and so forth; but if you are going to be suspended from school, the loss is less severe; therefore procedural due process becomes less formal.

Substantive Due Process

Perhaps the most important aspect of due process is substantive, which was first interpreted to apply to the substantive content or meaning of the law in 1923. The following definition by an Arizona court distinguished *substantive* due process from *procedural* due process:

> Due process, when applied to substantive rights, is interpreted to mean that the state is without right to deprive a person of Life, Liberty or property by an act that has no reasonable relation to any proper governmental purpose, or which is so far beyond the necessity of the case as to be an arbitrary exercise of governmental powers. (*Valley National Bank of Phoenix v. Glover,* 1945, 292)

Today both substantive and procedural due process apply to the relationship between government and students. The courts have given school officials extensive authority to establish and enforce rules and resolutions relating to standards of conduct. However, these rules and regulations must be exercised within the framework of the constitution and may be neither abitrary nor capricious, or they will be declared unconstitutional under substantive due process.

The substantive areas of due process are very important because only after a substantive issue of liberty or property has been affected would the school be required to give the student procedural due process. The court in speaking to this point said:

> The requirements of procedural due process apply only to the deprivation of interest encompassed by the Fourteenth Amendment's protection of liberty and property. When protected interests are implicated, the right of some kind of prior hearing is paramount. But the range of interests protected by procedural due process is not infinite. (*Board of Regents v. Roth,* 1972)

Therefore, the substantive aspects of due process are the foundation upon which due process is built.

The basic constitutional rights of students have a substantive origin found in the First, Fourth, Fifth, and Fourteenth amendments of the Constitution.

Some of these rights are freedom of; religion, speech, association, assembly, and other freedoms found in the Constitution that may be applied to students. One basic question about students' substantive rights is What are the liberty and property rights of public school students, and under what circumstances may these rights be limited by school authorities? This is an extremely important question because the federal courts will only intervene if a constitutional right has been violated.

A federal circuit court said: "For better or for worse, our jurisdiction attaches only when the Constitution has been violated—not every time a principal acts arbitrarily or unfairly" (*Murray v. West Baton Rouge Parish School Board,* 1973, 438). Two examples of substantive due process are the First Amendment right of freedom of expression and the Fourth Amendment freedom from unreasonable searches.

Tinker v. Des Moines was the landmark decision in the area of constitutional rights of students under the First Amendment. The Supreme Court, in referring to the student, said: "[H]e may express his opinions, even on controversial subjects . . . if he does so without materially and substantially interfering with the requirements of appropriate discipline in the operation of the school." The court further stated, "[T]he record does not demonstrate any facts which might reasonably have led school authorities to forecast substantial disruption of, or material interference with school activities."

There are two key elements in the language of the Supreme Court in *Tinker* relating to the substantive rights of students. First, the student does have substantive rights of freedom of expression guaranteed by the Constitution. Second, these substantive rights do have limits. The students' substantive rights may be limited if the "materially or substantially disrupt" the educational process or if disruption can be reasonably predicted by school officials.

The courts have refused to protect a student's substantive constitutional rights when the student's action disrupts the educational process. The courts have found for the school districts when students blocked hallways, threatened teachers, staged sit-ins, wore racially inciting patches or buttons, and engaged in many other actions of a similar nature.

It is now well established in law that students have a substantive right to freedom of expression, but it is equally well-established that these rights are limited if school officials can show disruption of the educational process or reasonably predict that such disruption is imminent. If a school principal or other officials attempt to restrict a student's activities and these activities are not disruptive and are protected by the constitution, then the official action may violate the student's substantive due process.

Another significant area of substantive due process for school officials is the Fourth Amendment to the Constitution, which states:

The right of the people to be secure in their persons, houses, papers, and effects, against *unreasonable* searches and seizures, shall not be violated, and no warrants shall issue, but upon probable cause, supported by oath or affirmation, and particularly describing the place to be searched and the persons or things to be seized. (Emphasis added)

The courts have ruled that it is reasonable for school officials to search students when the officials have "reasonable grounds" to believe that state laws or school regulations have been violated. If school officials have reasonable grounds, then the student's substantive rights are not violated by the Fourteenth Amendment's prohibition of unreasonable search. The courts have applied this reasoning and upheld school officials when they searched lockers, required students to empty the contents of their pockets, or searched a student's jacket, even though the student objected.

Although the substantive rights of the student under the Fourth Amendment have been recognized, the school has been given broader powers to limit the rights of students than under the First Amendment. One of the reasons for the difference is the interpretation of the two amendments in that a search and seizure usually involves dangerous weapons, illegal drugs, bomb threats, or other situations that may be hazardous to the health and safety of all school pupils, whereas first amendment situations may be disruptive but not of immediate harm to the student body.

Elements of Procedural Due Process

The basic concept of procedural due process is an opportunity to be heard in a fair manner, and the opportunity to establish the accuracy of the charges. Of course, as mentioned, the more serious the deprivation, the more formal the procedure for due process. A hearing for a student would be administrative in nature and would not provide all of the procedures established for criminal charges.

Although the process is flexible depending on the severity of charges, there are some basic elements of due process: there must be fair and reasonable *notice* of the charges; there must be an opportunity for a *hearing* and the hearing must be conducted by an *impartial tribunal;* that there is a *right to adult counsel* and there must be sufficient time to prepare for the hearing; the decision should be based on the *evidence* presented at the hearing.

Notice. Notice is the basic element of procedural due process and contains four stipulations. (1) The student must be forewarned of the type of conduct prohibited. A student is expected to know that violations of common social standards, such as fighting, are prohibited. But areas where rules and procedures are not common knowledge or of which it is reasonable for students not to be aware should be specified in a student handbook. A handbook gives students the forewarning they deserve to avoid violating uncommon rules or regulations. An example of a rule placed in a handbook because it would not be common knowledge would be the acceptable procedure that had been established by the school for distributing underground newspapers. (2) The student should be notified of what specific rule he has broken. The notification may be oral (see *Goss v. Lopez,* 1975) for less serious offenses but should be written for the more serious offenses that might lead to expulsion. (3) The student must be informed of the time and place of the hearing. This point also encompasses an adequate time to prepare. The hearing is not fundamentally fair unless the student has adequate time to prepare to refute the charges. (4) The student has the right to know the procedure that will be used for the hearing. Previous knowledge of exactly how the hearing will proceed allows for more adequate preparation.

As mentioned previously, all of the stipulations of notice may take place almost immediately for short-term suspension as outlined by *Goss;* but for more severe punishments, such as expulsion, the school should implement a more formal notice process.

The Hearing. The hearing must adhere to the basic elements of fair play and provide the student with an opportunity to refute the charges presented against him or her. Also, the student must be allowed to present at the hearing whatever evidence is germain to the charges.

Impartial Tribunal. The student has the right under procedural due process to have the hearing before an individual or group that is impartial. An individual should not be a trier of fact if he or she has been directly involved in the incident with which the student is charged. It is extremely important for the accused in receiving a fair hearing that those making the decision be impartial and have no preconceived ideas about accuracy of charges. (See for teacher *Hortonville Joint School Dist. No. 1 v. Hortonville Educ. Ass'n,* 1976.)

Right to Counsel. A student has a right to have his or her parents or some other adult at the hearing, but there is no right to be represented by legal counsel. The hearing is not a court of law but only an administrative process to ascertain the truth. If it were a basic right to have legal counsel, then all children would have to have access to legal counsel regardless of his or her economic condition. This would force the schools to provide an attorney for poor children at no cost. In *Goss* the court said that they were not going so far as to require legal counsel for short-term suspension. But at the same time, the door was left open by the court to require legal counsel if the situation required representation to maintain fundamental fairness. School districts throughout the country have policies that say a student may have legal counsel at a disciplinary hearing but at the expense of the student. However, this is a prerogative established by the school board. If the school district proceeds with counsel, then the child has a right to legal representation. (Public Law 94-142, the Education of the Handicapped, has different procedural due process for special education than that required for regular students.)

Witnesses. In *Goss* the Court did not go so far as to require the confrontation and cross-examination of witnesses for short-term suspension. A problem with witnesses is that many school boards throughout the country do not have subpoena power. With no subpoena power the student and school officials may ask the witnesses to attend and testify but there is no way to compel them to do so. If the testimony of one witness is the crucial factor in determining the outcome of the hearing, then the student has a right to cross-examine in this special circumstance so that fairness could be maintained.

Self-incrimination. The Fifth Amendment protects individuals from self-incrimination in criminal trials. But the amendment does not apply to students in administrative hearings. If students refuse to answer questions, they may not use the Fifth Amendment as protection, and the tribunal may interpret the nonanswer as they please.

Evidence. The evidence standards in an administrative hearing are not the same as those in a criminal trial. In criminal trials the evidence must be beyond a reasonable doubt, whereas in civil cases, there has to be a preponderance of evidence. In student disciplinary cases, the lower standard of preponderance of evidence would apply. Have the school officials presented sufficient evidence to support the alleged charges? Also, the hearing panel's decision can only be made from the evidence presented at the hearing; other facts obtained previously or outside of the hearing should not enter into the final disposition of the hearing.

Since the hearing is administrative, the formal rules of evidence do not apply. The panel or individual hearing the alleged charges is free to hear whatever evidence either party chooses to present. Hearsay evidence has been allowed in student disciplinary cases, but it must be placed in the total context of the hearing.

Double Jeopardy. Students have claimed double jeopardy when they have been arrested in the local government jurisdiction for drugs and also face school disciplinary charges based on the same incident. Double jeopardy only applies in criminal proceedings and only when the drug charges are against federal or state criminal statutes. Double jeopardy does not apply to administrative disciplinary hearings.

Academic Due Process

Procedural due process is required for children being removed from school for disciplinary reasons. But is procedural due process required for academic matters? The United States Supreme Court in *Board of Curators of the University of Missouri v. Horowitz* (1978, 952, 955) said,

> [I]n *Goss v. Lopez,* we held that due process requires, in connection with the suspension of a student from public school for *disciplinary* reasons, that the student be given oral or written notice of the charges against him and, if he denies them, an explanation of the evidence the authorities have and an opportunity to present his side of the story. . . . *Academic evaluations* of a student, in contrast to disciplinary determinations, bear little resemblance to the judicial and administrative fact finding proceedings.

The court determined that due process for academic matters is not required because grades and other academic matters are in the domain of the trained experts, the academicians. "[T]he determination to dismiss a student for academic reasons requires an expert evaluation of cumulative information and is not readily adapted to the procedural tools of judicial or administrative decision making" (Board of Curators, 1978, 955).

The United States Fourth Circuit Court of Appeals, citing *Horowitz,* upheld a school board, superintendent, principal, and teacher when the teacher did not promote 22 of 23 second-grade students to the third grade. The school officials said the children had not completed a reading series, although they could read on the third-grade level. The court determined because of *Horowitz* that the evaluation of academic issues is an inappropriate subject for court review and should be left to the academians. Therefore, grades, promotions, and other academic areas do not come under the scrutiny of the courts; they are left to the academicians as long as their actions are not arbitrary, capricious, or discriminatory against a protected class (*Sandlin v. Johnson,* 1980).

CHAPTER GUIDELINES

1. Students who are suspended or expelled from public schools must be given due process because attending school is considered a property right.
2. The more serious the offense the more formal due process should be.
3. A student generally would not have a right to legal counsel in an administrative hearing.
4. Due process is not required for academic situations that are non-discriminatory.

5. The federal court in *Dixon v. Alabama* described due process of "fundamental fairness."

SITUATIONAL DISCUSSIONS

Situation 1: As a school counselor, why is it important that you understand procedural due process? Discuss times when you might be expected to deal with this topic.

Situation 2: Contrast the terms *expulsion* and *suspension* from school.

Situation 3: Summarize what the courts said about short term school suspension and due process.

Situation 4: Define *substantive* and *procedural* due process.

Situation 5: Is procedural due process required for academic matters? Why is it important that school counselors understand this topic? When might counselors be called upon to deal with procedural due process concerning academic issues?

LEGAL REFERENCES

Board of Curators of University of Missouri v. Horowitz, 98 S.Ct. 948 (1978).
Board of Regents v. Roth, 408 U.S. 564 (1972).
Brown v. Board of Education of Topeka, 347 U.S. 483, (1954).
Dixon v. Alabama State Board of Education 294 F.2d 150; Cert. den. 82 S.Ct. 368 (5th Cir. 1961).
Goss v. Lopez, 419 U.S. 565, 95 S.Ct. 729 (1975).
Gott v. Berea College, 161 S.W. 204 (1913).
Hortonville Joint School Dist. No. 1 v. Hortonville Educ. Ass'n., 426, U.S. 482, 96 S.Ct. 2308 (1976).
Murray v. West Baton Rouge Parish School Board, 472 F.2d 438 (5th Cir. 1973).
Public Law 94-142, The Education of the Handicapped, 20 USC § 1400 et seq.
Sandlin v. Johnson, 643 F.2d 1027 (4th Cir. 1980).
Tinker v. Des Moines, 393 U.S. 503 (1969)
U.S. Constitution, First, Fourth, Tenth, and Fourteenth amendments.
Valley National Bank of Phoenix v. Glover 159 P2d 292 (Sup. C. Ariz. 1945).

Chapter 8

Client Records

Records pertaining to students have been kept since schools first opened in this country. These records were commonly called student registers and contained the names of pupils, dates of enrollment and withdrawal, citations of promotion to higher grades, and any disciplinary actions taken. State funds were allocated based on these registers to verify the number of pupils attending school.

Two major educational movements stimulated the increase in student record keeping: the scientific movement and the whole-child concept. The scientific movement was brought about by the development of more elaborate and intricate measuring devices. These instruments were used to better evaluate the child and, therefore, provide a better educational program. Because more data were collected, the record-keeping process began to expand. The second movement, although not mutually exclusive of the first, was the whole-child concept. Educational philosophies were changing from teaching the child just the basic skills to dealing with and understanding the whole child socially, emotionally, and physically. More sophisticated techniques of measuring each facet of the child were developed and this, correspondingly, produced more comprehensive documents.

Privacy is not specifically mentioned in the federal Constitution. With the increase of technology, individuals became more concerned about the types of information being maintained by government. With the development of computers, there was a growing apprehension concerning the privacy of the individual in society. (see *Mapp v. Ohio,* 1961). This same apprehension has caused concern about the use of social security numbers for identification. Some states passed legislation similar to that in Virginia stating:

> After July 1, 1973 it shall be unlawful for any agency to require an individual to disclose or furnish his social security account number not previously disclosed or furnished, for any purpose in connection with any activity, or to refuse any service, privilege or right to an individual wholly or partly because such individual does not disclose or furnish such number, unless the disclosure of such number is specifically required by federal or state law. (Code of Virginia, 1950)

In 1968, a report of the House Special Subcommittee on the computer and invasion of privacy stated: "information can be too treacherous, a commodity to be widely disseminated with ineffectual controls. Even a little information, improperly used, can do irrevocable harm" ("The Computer and Invasion of Privacy," 1968, 121-122).

The courts (*Mapp v. Ohio,* 1961) have recognized the individuals right of privacy in society. But privacy rights have not been extended to children attending public schools. Although students have constitutional rights (*Tinker v. Des Moines,* 1969) these are not coextensive with the rights of individuals in society (see *People v. D.,* 1974, 466, 468). Therefore, the privacy rights of students are not as great as those of the individual in society.

In *Merriken v. Cressman* (1976), the school district wanted to identify children who were potential drug abusers and to prepare intervention programs. The students claimed the type of information the schools were seeking was an invasion of privacy. The court ruled the information was an invasion of familial privacy, which is distinguishable from the individual privacy of the student.

The Russell Sage Foundation conducted a study in 1968 and found that school officials were releasing personally identifiable information to other governmental agencies, such as police departments, but would not release the same information to the parents. This, and other studies, caused considerable concern among parents about their rights to see their children's school records.

Parents sought judicial relief and began to challenge school officials, seeking access to their childrens' records. In *Van Allen v. McCleary* (1961, 501), the Supreme Court of Nassau County said:

> Petitioners rights, if any, stem not from his status as taxpayer seeking to review the records of a public corporation, but from his relationship with school authorities as a parent under compulsory education. Thus, the common law rule . . . that when not detrimental to the public interest, . . . as a matter of law, the parent is entitled to inspect the records.

Various advocacy groups began to inform legislators of the problems concerning student records, as perceived by parents and others. In 1974 Congress passed federal legislation permitting parents and students access to public school records.

THE FAMILY EDUCATIONAL RIGHTS AND PRIVACY ACT

The Family Educational Rights and Privacy Act was enacted by the United States Congress on August 21, 1974, and became effective November 19, 1974. The act is commonly known as "the Buckley Amendment" for its originator, Senator James Buckley of New York. When this legislation was originally written and passed, it was designed for elementary and secondary schools. But because the terminology *educational institution* was used, it was applicable to institutions of higher education; and certain provisions that were inappropriate have been amended.

In a rather unusual move, the legislation was not referred to committee for hearings and was introduced directly on the floor of the Senate. Senator Buckley preferred not to have it considered by committee, because his only aim was to protect students and he believed the education committees would not be receptive to the legislation (see *School Law News,* 1974).

What Is an Educational Record?

The act applies to any educational institution, either public or private, receiving federal funds. Educational records are not directly defined by the statute but are defined through exclusion. Educational records are any records except records of instructional personnel and supervisory and administrative staff. Therefore, they are not personnel records, or the records of employees, but are the student records kept by the institution. Employee records are generally covered by state statutes, and employees would normally have access to these through state statutes such as the freedom of information acts or sunshine laws.

Student records in the sole possession of the maker do not fall under the jurisdiction of this the "Buckley Amendment." If guidance counselors are maintaining records used solely for the purpose of "jogging the counselor's memory" concerning an individual child, they are excluded from the act. But if the guidance counselor shares these records with other personnel except a qualified substitute, then these individual notes become a part of the official student record.

The law specifies that law enforcement records, which are kept separate from the regular records, are not a part of the educational records. If the records of law enforcement officials such as campus police and probation officers are kept on campus, they are not covered by the act. But if these records are mingled with educational records or if school officials have access to these records, they become a part of the student's educational records.

If a student is 18 years old or older or attending a postsecondary institution and records are maintained by school employees such as a physician, psychiatrist, psychologist, another professional, or a paraprofessional for the sole purpose of treating a student, then these treatment records are not a part of the educational records. Although the individual does not have direct access to these treatment records, the student may have those records examined by an appropriate professional from outside of the institution as selected by the student.

The act provides some specific areas of exclusion for students attending postsecondary institutions. Students attending a postsecondary institution do not have access to the following records:

1. The financial records of the parents or any financial information concerning parents.
2. Any letters of recommendation or confidential letters that were written before January 1, 1975. These letters are confidential as long as they are used for the purposes for which they were originally intended.
3. If students sign a waiver, then they have waived their right of access. Student waivers only apply if the letters are being used as the students originally intended. If letters or information are being used in a manner other than which the students intended, then the waivers no longer apply. Students may waive their right to confidential information used for admission purposes to educational institutions. Although the students have waived their right to see the letters of recommendation, they may still request and obtain the names of people writing confidential letters. Students may freely waive their right to see the letters of recommendation, but no institution may condition admission, financial aid, or the receipt of any other beneficial service based upon the precondition that a waiver must be instituted.

Only records kept on the student while they are matriculating are covered by the act. The statute does not apply to the records kept by institutions concerning alumni. If the institution has a graduate who becomes very successful and receives much public attention, and the institution keeps press clippings as a part of alumni activities, these are not defined as part of the educational records. Also, the act covers all present and former students, but if state law does not require particular records to be kept, they may be expunged.

Directory Information

The educational institution may provide directory information to the public but only after the student or his parents have been notified of the type of information to be released. The student or parent must have an opportunity to request no directory information be released. Directory information is defined as the student's name, address, telephone number, date and place of birth, major field of study, participation in officially recognized activities and sports, weight and height of members of athletic teams, dates of attendance, degrees and awards received, and the most recent previous educational agency or institution attended by the students.

Access to Information

The basic aspect of the federal legislation is to allow parents and students access to educational records. The institution must inform the parents or students of all records that are maintained. The parents, or student, have a right to inspect the records and request explanations or interpretation of such records. If after the explanation, the parents or student are not satisfied, they may challenge the records if they believe the records are inaccurate or misleading. The individual may request a due process hearing. After an inpartial trier of the fact hears the case, a decision is rendered to leave the records as they are or to expunge the challenged section. If the parents disagree, then they may attach their explanation to the records. The information in the records does not have to be deleted if the information is true, factual, and school authorities believe it to be germaine to the education of the student. Individuals have queried: does this statute give the individual the right to challenge a grade? The parents could challenge the grade if it were *incorrectly* recorded but not to refute the grade. Grades and the grading policies are the discretion of the educator as long as they are not capricious or arbitrary (see *Board of Curators of University of Missouri v. Horowitz,* 1978).

Education agencies must establish rules and regulations as to the appropriate procedure for allowing access to education records. Agencies must allow access within 45 days of the request and cannot destroy or change records after the request has been made and prior to the inspection by parents.

Access by Third Parties

There are certain third parties as specified by statute who have access to student information without written permission from the student or parent.

Information may be released to school officials or teachers within the local educational district who have a need for such information. Appropriate personnel would be individuals who are in a position to benefit the child and his education. Also, school officials of other school districts where the student intends to enroll may receive the records without prior written permission But before the information is released to another school district, the student's parents must be notified.

Certain governmental officials, or their representatives, may have access to student records, without written permission, for the purpose of determining whether federal or state programs are adhering to specified guidelines. These include the comptroller general of the United States, the secretary of education, and state educational authorities. Also, state or federal officials may have access to the records when students have made application for financial assistance. Any state or local official who was authorized to receive student information by state statute before November 19, 1974, may continue to receive information.

Organizations acting on behalf of educational agencies or institutions may receive student information for the purpose of validating tests, improving instruction, or administering student aid. But these organizations may not receive information that is personally identifiable. Accrediting organizations may receive information to carry out their role of accreditation.

One of the areas that has come under discussion is at what age and under what conditions are students emancipated and totally free to receive their records, exclusive of their parents? The federal statute provides that permission, or consent, required from the parents is transferred to the students when they reach 18 or are attending a postsecondary institution. But there is one exception. If the parents of the student are providing for over one-half of his or her financial support, under section 157 of the Internal Revenue Code of 1954, then they may receive student record information. Generally, it would be at the school's discretion whether to allow the parents access to the records, but the school would have the authority to do so if the parents are still the main source of financial support for the student.

A provision of the act specifies student information may be released to third parties in case of an emergency such as an epidemic. It would be important for the institution to be able to prove that the information was released to someone who had the power to deal appropriately with such an emergency.

CASES

Parents challenged the procedures Mississippi was using in placing handicapped children in specialized classes (*Mattie T. v. Johnston,* 1976). A subpoena was issued to a school official to give testimony and produce documents named in the subpoena. The school officials did not appear and disobeyed the subpoena because the children's legal counsel did not assure the school officials that applicable provisions of the Family Educational Rights and Privacy Act would be adhered to before the documents were submitted. The Mississippi District Court found that "the Act does not bar the disclosure of the subpoenaed documents under the conditions provided in the subpoena" (*Mattie T.,* 1976, 501). The court also noted the act provides information shall be furnished "in compliance with judicial order, or pursuant to any lawfully issued subpoena" (p. 501) provided the parents are notified before compliance with the judicial decrees. The court determined that documents had to be produced within 10 days or the officials would be in contempt and

> that all personally identifiable information, as that term is defined in the Family Educational Rights and Privacy Act of 1974, and the regulations implementing said Act, shall be deleted, covered up, or made at least temporarily unreadable prior to the production of the subpoenaed documents. (*Mattie T.,* 1976, 503)

In a medical malpractice suit, the plaintiff requested information concerning the physician's medical training. The physician had apparently not completed his residency and plaintiff wanted the records from the medical school to confirm this fact. The physician claimed the Family Educational Rights and Privacy Act bestowed a privilege, and therefore records were not accessible. The federal court stated:

> In the instant case, defendants have failed to meet their burden. The statute relied upon relates to "privacy" and would appear to establish procedures for advising or notifying a person when educational records pertaining to said person are to be released pursuant to a judicial order. The court determines that the information sought does not appear to be privileged pursuant to rules of evidence. (*Reeg v. Fetzer,* 1976, 34)

In 1981, a newspaper publisher filed suit against an intercollegiate athletic conference to determine the amount of money member institutions dispersed to student athletes. The Arkansas Intercollegiate Athletic Conference (AIC) had records for each student athlete for the amount paid him through athletic conference grant; the amount loaned to the student; the amount paid the student from federal and state grants, that is, Basic Educational Opportunity Grant (BEOG); the amount paid through other grants; the financial aid given to him; and any notes the student may have signed and their amount. The Arkansas Supreme Court determined that the records were neither "scholastic records" under the Arkansas Freedom of Information Act or "educational records" under the Family Educational Rights and Privacy Act of 1974. The only thing that was covered by the federal act was the students applications for grants and loans that are confidential. In summation, the court said:

> The AIC is not an educational agency or institution subject to the authority of the Federal Commission of Education as defined by the act, §1232g (a) (3), and is not subject to the act. However, the member institutions are subject to the authority of the Commission and they have been supplying records to the AIC which conceivably are "educational records" which are "personally identifiable" as described by §1232g (a) (4) (A). If the colleges and universities have breached the federal act that breach has already occurred and those member institutions cannot now claim that they should not have supplied the information to the AIC. The records sought are not required by law to be closed to the public. (*Arkansas Gazette Co. v. Southern State College,* 1981, 758)

In another case, a 14-year old was murdered, and criminal charges were brought against the defendant (*State v. Birdsall,* 1977). The defendant claimed self-defense, intoxication, and insanity. A motion was made by the defendant's counsel for the disclosure of the deceased victim's junior high school records. The Arizona lower court ordered the school guidance counselor to appear in court with the victim's school records. The school board, arguing the subpoena was too broad, moved for a protective order or a modification. The Arizona appellate court determined the subpoena was too broad; but because the defendant claimed self-defense, the scholastic records could be excluded, but all disciplinary records had to be produced. The purpose of producing the disciplinary records was to determine the deceased victim's reputation as an aggressor. The state claimed federal privacy prohibited it from producing the records. But the court said:

> First of all, as to the federal statute, it should be noted that it prohibits a practice or policy of disclosure of educational records except in designated instances, and expressly recognizes that disclosure may be made in response to a subpoena *duces tecum* or other judicial order. Responsibility for notification of parents and student is placed upon educational institutions and not on the person seeking disclosure of the records. Thus we conclude that the state's reliance upon the federal statute is misplaced. (*State v. Birdsall,* 1977, 1097)

In 1976 a student brought suit, claiming misconduct on the part of the University of San Francisco for releasing grades previously earned at Columbia University to the State Scholarship and Loan Commission (*Porten v. University of San Francisco,* 1976). The University of San Francisco had assured him the grades would only be used for the purposes of evaluating his application and remain confidential thereafter. Because one of the allegations by the student was an invasion of privacy, grounded in tort theory, the California court of appeals stated the

> four distinct forms of tortious invasion of privacy [are]: (1) the commercial appropriation of the plaintiff's name or likeness; (2) intrusion upon the plaintiff's physical solitude or seclusion; (3) publicity which places the plaintiff in a false light in the public eye; and (4) public disclosure of true embarrassing private facts about the plaintiff. (*Porten,* 1976, 839)

The court found that the private facts disclosed had not been disclosed to the public and dismissed the tort claim. The court did recognize the right of privacy in student records (see The Family Educational Rights and Privacy Act, 1974), and the student had presented a prima facie violation of his right of privacy under state constitutional provision.

CHAPTER GUIDELINES

1. The constitutional rights of students in public schools are not as coextensive as the rights of individuals in society.
2. The Family Educational Rights and Privacy Act allows students the right to inspect their student records in any institution that receives federal funds.
3. If records are kept by counselors to "jog" their memories, then these are excluded from the definition of being student records.
4. Students may waive their rights to see letters of recommendation but may not be required to do so as a condition of participation.
5. A school may release directory information about a student, but first must give the student the opportunity to refuse such release.
6. The court may subpoena student records if it is of vital interest to the parties involved in litigation.

SITUATIONAL DISCUSSIONS

Situation 1: Discuss the impact of the Family Educational Rights and Privacy Act on record keeping in schools. Have the overall effects been positive or negative? Explain.

Situation 2: Identify some third parties having access to student records without permission of the student or parent.

Situation 3: Determine if your state has a statute pertaining to student records. Compare the statute to the federal statute.

Situation 4: In cases involving divorced parents, who has access to the child's record? Explain.

LEGAL REFERENCES

Arkansas Gazette Co. v. Southern State College, 620 S.W.2d 758 (S. C. Ark. 1981)
Board of Curators of University of Missouri v. Horowitz 98 S. Ct. 948 (1978).
Code of Virginia, 1950, § 2.1-385.
The computer and invasion of privacy, 1968, Committee on Government Operations, Subcommittee, United States Congress, Hearing, 89th Congress, 2nd Session July 26, 27, 28, pp. 121-122.
The Family Educational Rights and Privacy Act, 1974, P.L.93.380, 20 U.S.C. § 1239g
Mapp v. Ohio, 367 U.S. 643, 81 S.Ct. 1684 (1961).
Mattie T. v. Johnston, 74 F.R.D. 498 (N.D. Miss. 1976).
Merriken v. Cressman, 364 F.Supp. 913. (E.D. Pa. 1976).
People v. D., 315 N.E.2d 466, (N.Y. 1974).
Porten v. University of San Francisco, 134 Cal. Rptr. 839 (1976).
Reeg v. Fetzer, 78 F.R.D. 34 (W.D. Okla. 1976).
School Law News, 1974, (November 13), Capital Publications, Washington, D.C.
State v. Birdsall, 568 P.2d 1094 (Ariz. 1977).
Tinker v. Des Moines, 393 U.S. 503, 89 S.Ct. 733 (1969).
University of Missouri v. Horowitz, 98 S.Ct. 948 (1978).
Van Allen v. McCleary, 211 N.Y.S.2d 501. (S. C. Nassau County, 1961).

Chapter 9

Educational Testing and Placement

Historically, standardized test scores have been used to identify individuals for educational placement and to develop educational programs. Unfortunately, standardized tests have been misused. The problem lies in the difficulty in classifying individuals correctly. First, test results have often been misinterpreted, which has resulted in discrimination against certain types of students. Second, testing instruments themselves, standardized on samples of white middle-class students, have discriminated against the emotionally disadvantaged, the handicapped, and racial minorities.

Shea (1977) explained that educators have failed to distinguish between *genotype, phenotype,* and *operative intelligence,* which has led to misapplication of tests (p. 145). Shea defined genotype intelligence as "innate genetic potential." Phenotype intelligence was defined as the interaction between environmental forces with genotype intelligence (p. 138). Operative intelligence was described as behavior that can be measured on tests (p. 139). Shea concluded:

> As intelligence tests primarily measure operative, rather than genotype intelligence, the use of these test scores as indicators of genotype intelligence must be carefully limited in order to be valid . . . Too often persons have construed intelligence tests as measuring innate intelligence without control of these environmental factors. (1977, 147)

Selected portions of this chapter are used with permission from L. C. Talbutt, 1983, The counselor and testing: some legal concerns, *The School Counselor* **30:**245-250.

Kamin (1975) wrote, "Since its introduction to America, the intelligence test has been used more or less as an instrument of oppression against the underprivileged—the poor, the foreign-born and racial minorities" (p. 317). Because tests may discriminate, individuals should not be classified or grouped solely on standardized and intelligence test scores. McCarthy and Thomas (1977) suggested that educational placement be based on a substantial variety of data, not merely test scores. They wrote, "Anecdotal, historical records, direct observation, testing, and pupil-parent conferences should be utilized" (p. 51).

To prevent discrimination, counselors, psychologists, and other professionals should understand laws relating to testing and placement and should be knowledgeable of ways in which discrimination can occur. Additionally, counselors should follow recommendations provided through professional literature and professional standards.

PUBLIC LAWS

Several public laws have addressed discrimination in education. Public Law 93-380, the Elementary and Secondary Amendments of 1974, declared that all children have equal educational opportunities. "All children enrolled in public schools are entitled to equal educational opportunity without regard to race, color, sex, or national origin" (88 Stat. 514).

Sex discrimination was addressed under title IX in Public Law 92-318, known as the Education Amendments of 1972. "Sec.901(a) No person in the United States shall, on the basis of sex, be excluded from participation in, be denied the benefits of, or be subjected to discrimination under any education program or activity receiving Federal assistance" (86 Stat. 373).

Major laws have also dealt with discrimination of the handicapped. Hohenshil and Humes (1979) pointed out that more than 200 federal laws have been adopted since 1827 to deal with the handicapped. They concluded that two pieces of current legislation are landmarks in this field, Public Law 93-112 and Public Law 94-142 (p. 222). Public Law 93-112, the Rehabilitation Act of 1973, called attention to the human rights of the handicapped. Sections 503 and 504 mandated equal opportunities for the handicapped regarding "employment, education, transportation, housing, and accessibility" (Brolin and Gysbers, 1979, 259). Public Law 94-142, the Education for all Handicapped Children Act of 1975, was created to assure that all handicapped children have a free and appropriate public education.

> It is the purpose of this act to assure that all handicapped children have available to them . . . a free appropriate public education which emphasizes special education and related services designed to meet their unique needs, to assure that the rights of handicapped children and their parents or guardians are protected. (89 Stat. 775)

The law has also addressed the area of discrimination in testing and placement of pupils for special education classes.

> Procedures to assure that testing and evaluation materials and procedures utilized for the purposes of evaluation and placement of handicapped children will be selected and administered so as not to be racially or culturally discriminatory . . . No single procedure shall be the sole criterion for determining an appropriate education program for a child. (89 Stat. 781)

The major federal laws quoted in this chapter clearly show that all children are entitled to appropriate and free public education regardless of their race, handicap, sex, or nationality. Further, public law makes it clear that testing and placement programs should not discriminate against certain types of students. Besides knowing federal laws, counselors, psychologists, and other helping professionals should understand relevant court cases and their legal implications to avoid discrimination in testing and placement.

CASES

In *Brown v. Board of Education* (1954), the United States Supreme Court determined that when a state makes public education available, "It is a right which must be made available to all on equal terms" (p. 493). Since the historical court decision, the courts have dealt with many examples of discrimination, including race and handicaps, resulting from testing and placement.

Testing instruments themselves often lead to discrimination. In *Hobson v. Hansen* (1967) the U.S. District Court ruled that ability tracking in the District of Columbia, "[u]nconstitutionally deprived Negro and poor public school children of their right to equal educational opportunity" (p. 401). The court analyzed the use of standardized aptitude tests in the tracking of students and concluded that test produced inaccurate and misleading scores.

> Because these tests are standardized primarily on and are relevant to a white middle class group of students, they produce inaccurate and misleading test scores when given to lower class and Negro students. As a result . . . these students are in reality being classified according to their socio-economic or racial status, or—more precisely—according to environmental and psychological factors which have nothing to do with innate ability. (P. 514)

In support of the conclusion, one of the principal findings stated by the court was that "Racially and socially homogeneous schools damage the minds and spirit of all children who attend them—the Negro, the white, and the poor and the affluent—and block the attainment of the broader goals of democratic education, whether the segregation occurs by law or by fact" (*Hobson,* 1967, 406).

The courts have held that students may not be placed in classrooms according to standardized ability and achievement tests when this method serves to perpetuate segregated classrooms in recently desegregated schools. To use tests in this way is a violation of the Fourteenth Amendment rights of black students, according to *Moses v. Washington Parish School Board* (1972).

Test scores have often been misinterpreted by educators. McCarthy and Thomas (1977) identified special education assignments as a crucial area because incorrect classification of a student could have harmful psychological effects (p. 82). *Hoffman v. Board of Education* (1978) illustrates a case dealing with misclassifications. A student was just below the cutoff point according to an intelligence test used to place pupils in a special classroom setting; thus, the school psychologists had recommended reevaluation within two years. The school board failed to follow the recommendation. The N.Y. Supreme Court of appeals reversed the lower court's decision, ruled in favor of the school board, and determined that the court should not interfere with the professional judgment of those involved in educational settings unless "gross violations" have occurred. While many individuals would personally view the *Hoffman* case as an example of gross violation, the court upheld the traditional view that the courts should not interfere in academic decisions in educational settings unless absolutely necessary. The case, nevertheless, illustrates the harmful results of classifying a student with borderline test scores according to a single evaluation.

McCarthy and Thomas (1977) identified *Pennsylvania Association for Retarded Children (P.A.R.C.) v. Commonwealth* (1972) as "the first notable case involving the rights of handicapped children" (p. 77). In that case the court determined that no mentally handicapped student could be denied a public education or procedural due process of law. The Eastern District Court of Pennsylvania concluded: "due process required hearing before retarded children could be denied public education and that state, having undertaken to provide public education to some children, could not deny it to retarded children entirely" (P.A.R.C., 1972, 279).

In another case, *Mills v. Board of Education* (1972), the court made a decision similar to *P.A.R.C. v. Commonwealth.* However, the right to an education was expanded to those other than the mentally retarded. *Mills* held that "children who had been labeled as behavioral problems, mentally retarded, emotionally disturbed, or hyperactive" could not be denied a public education (p. 866). The court decided that denying these children an education while providing one for other children directly violated the Fifth Amendment of the United States Constitution. Furthermore, the court held that the expense involved was not sufficient reason for denying handicapped pupils a public education. The conclusion of *Mills* was that no child could be "excluded from a regular public school assignment . . . unless adequate alternative educational services . . . and a constitutionally adequate prior hearing" were provided (p. 872).

Testing instruments should be both reliable and free from discrimination. A Virginia case, *Copeland v. School Board of City of Portsmouth* (1972), made a statement regarding the reliability of tests. The Eastern District Court of Virginia concluded: "It is essential that the record establish that the tests and examinations used in making assignments are relevant, reliable and free of discrimination" (*Copeland*, 1972, 934).

The courts have determined that tests should be valid. In other words, there should be a relationship between what the test measures and the job to be performed or the subject matter taught. The court, in *Griggs v. Duke Power Co.* (1971), ruled that requiring a high school diploma or a particular score on an intelligence test violated title VII of the Civil Rights Act of 1964. The court concluded that neither the diploma nor the test requirement had a relationship to successful work performance (p. 431).

An area of testing currently receiving a great deal of publicity is minimum competency. Basically, minimum competency means that certain standards are mandated by the state in order for students to graduate or be promoted. The topic of minimum competency is probably of more concern to administrators than counselors. However, the topic is included because the pros and cons of competency testing is widely discussed in professional literature and the issue has been addressed by the courts.

In *Debra P. v. Turlington* (1981), a Florida circuit court determined that a state has a right to require certain standards on a test for high school diplomas. The real issues in the case were whether or not the past education of black students in desegregated schools discriminated against their chances of passing the test and whether or not the test was valid. In other words, did the test cover curricula taught in the Florida schools, and were all students exposed to the same curriculum. The court of appeals stated: "We hold that the State may not constitutionally so deprive its students unless it has submitted proof of the curricular validity of the test" (*Debra P.,* 1981, 397). Pullin (1981) wrote that the challenge to Florida's minimum competency testing "was not a challenge to testing *per se,* not even a challenge to minimum competency testing *per se* . . . [instead it] challenged the manner in which [the testing] was implemented" (p. 20). In conclusion, the appeals court in Florida agreed with the lower court that a state has a right to set test standards for graduation and agreed to the four year delay in using the test. However, the appeals court determined that the test should be fair (should cover material taught) and that the state must show or prove the validity of the test.

Minimum competency is an issue for boards of education, administrators, testing committees and authors, and state departments of education. Counselors may have indirect responsibilities for minimum competency testing. For example, counselors may serve on committees or supervise the administration of tests for minimum competency testing. However, all counselors, whether working in an institution or in private practice, should be concerned about the validity of any test given. According to *Ethical Standards of the American Personnel and Guidance Association* (APGA) (1981), counselors should "consider carefully [test] validity."

THE COUNSELING PROCESS

Counselors and others in the helping professions should be aware that discrimination may occur in the counseling process by words and actions as well as through counseling materials. Regarding sex discrimination in the counseling process, *University of Pennsylvania Law Review* (1976) stated the following: "Some of the more subtle and destructive sex discrimination in education takes place in the area of counseling. The effect on a young girl of a counselor's saying that a given career is inappropriate for her can be irreversible" (pp. 828-829).

That review indicated that title IX of the Education Amendments of 1972 calls for counselors to use the same tests in evaluating students of different sexes. When one sex dominates a particular program or class, schools are expected to examine the counseling program to be sure there is no discrimination based on sex bias in counseling, tests, or materials (*University of Pennsylvania,* 1976, 828-829).

Counselors should examine carefully all materials they use to be sure no discrimination exists. In addition, counselors should examine their own biases regarding race, sex, or handicap and deal fairly and objectively with all clients. There are times when counselors recommend that clients seek help from other professionals. Referral is necessary when counselors' bias prevent them from being objective.

Public Law 92-318, Education Amendments of 1972 quoted earlier, addressed sex discrimination under title IX. Interpretations of title IX include directions for counselors in dealing with sex discrimination. The Project on Equal Education Rights (PEER, 1972, 2) adopted a summary related to sex roles in education, based on material prepared by the Resource Center on Sex Roles in Education of the National Foundation for the Improvement of Education. The summary included a section on counseling as it relates to the treatment of students.

A recipient may not discriminate on the basis of sex in counseling or guiding students.

Whenever a school finds that a class has a disproportionate number of students of one sex, it must take whatever action is necessary to assure that sex bias in counseling or testing is not responsible.

A recipient may not use tests or other appraisal and counseling materials which use different materials for each sex or which permit or require different treatment for students of each sex. Exceptions can be made if different materials used for each sex cover the same occupations and they are essential to eliminate sex bias.

Schools must set up their own procedures to make certain that counseling and appraisal materials are not sex-biased. If a test does result in a substantially disproportionate number of students of one sex in a course of study or classification, the school must take action to ensure that bias in the test or its application is not causing the disproportion. (PEER, 1972, 2)

A Virginia assistant attorney general commented on title IX and its effect on education in *Attorney General's Conference on School Law, Transcript of Proceedings* (Ryland, 1975, 46-57). Specific recommendations were made for counselors.

You are required to develop "internal procedures for assuring that test materials are nondiscriminatory." This means that if you give a different aptitude test to girls and boys, this is bad. If your aptitude tests are showing that all of your girls ought to be nurses or girls' physical education teachers or seek traditional women's occupations, then you are supposed to undertake to determine whether your tests are valid. The regulations say, where the use of a counseling test results in a disproportionate number of one sex in a course, the recipients shall insure that the result is not due to discrimination in the test. In other words, if your placement procedures are getting most of the girls in home economics, and most of the boys in shop, you have to make sure that your placement procedures are not inherently discriminatory. (P. 49)

Sex bias also exists in counseling materials. In three original studies, Harway (1977) found that sex bias exists in achievement tests and interest inventories. Harway found sex bias in textbooks and vocational handbooks for counselors as well as college catalogs (p. 57). Harway explained that work is being done on tests and other materials but noted that change is slow. Harway recommended, "In the interim, *it is the counselors' responsibility to raise questions about every tool they use.*" Counselors should "take steps to counteract the stereotypical assumptions of any materials" (Harway, 1977, 63). Engelhard, Jones, and Striggins (1976) challenged guidance counselors to deal with sex role biases and made the following recommendations for counselors who want to be supportive of women. Counselors must "(1) recognize the changing roles of women in American society, (2) recognize and evaluate his own sex role biases and (3) develop some level of expertise with the growing body of recent research on sex differences and on the psychology of women" (p. 365).

Moore and Strickler (1980) wrote, "The decade of the 1970's has seen a growing awareness of and commitment to the belief that nonsexist counseling is necessary for the optimal growth of clients" (p. 86). Still, they found a discrepancy between the support in the professional literature and training and continuing educational programs. They concluded that emphasis should now be placed upon "training and renewal programs so that concepts of sex equity receive due attention and reach into all corners of training and practice" (p. 86). Bernard and Gilliland (1981) emphasized that counselors should adhere to the ethical standards that require counselors to respect each client as an individual. They concluded, "The ethical counselor should be free of sex-biased behavior" (p. 39).

Counselors, psychologists, and others in the helping professions should avoid all acts of discrimination. The following questions should help counselors evaluate themselves regarding discrimination:

1. Is the counseling process free from subtle discriminations in attitudes, speech, vocational expectations, and placement?
2. Have I as a counselor evaluated my own bias regarding race, sex, or handicaps? When I am biased, do I make referrals?
3. Do I as a counselor evaluate all counseling materials, information, and tests for discrimination? Do I avoid such materials?
4. Do I as a counselor keep up with new research, professional literature, and programs concerning discrimination?
5. Do I as a counselor follow ethical standards, and am I ethical in all of my dealings with clients?

RECOMMENDATIONS FOR TESTING

The previous court cases and laws indicate that counselors should use valid and reliable tests and should be cautious when making interpretations regarding minorities. Both APGA *Ethical Standards* (1981) and "Ethical Principles of Psychologists" (1981) address testing and are consistent with the previously discussed laws and court cases. *Ethical Standards* (1981) recommends that counselors refer to the *Standards for Educational and Psychological Tests and Manuals* (1974) regarding the preparation, publication, and distribution of tests.

Counselors should note that section C of *Ethical Standards* deals with measurement and evaluation. Section C-2 relates to test usage and C-10 relates to testing and minority students.

C:2 In selecting tests for use in a given situation or with a particular client, the member must consider carefully the specific validity, reliability, and appropriateness of the test(s). General validity, reliability and the like may be questioned legally as well as ethically when tests are used for vocational and educational selection, placement, or counseling. (P. 2)

C:10 The member must proceed with caution when attempting to evaluate and interpret the performance of minority group members or other persons who are not represented in the norm group on which the instrument was standardized. (P. 3)

In section C-2 validity refers to the extent to which a particular test measures what it purports to measure, whereas reliability refers to a test's stability. In administering tests counselors should carefully review all test manuals and follow all instructions. Although much information about a particular test can be found in a publisher's test manual, counselors should check the latest edition of Buro's *Mental Measurements Yearbook* (1978) for a complete evaluation. The yearbook indicates if machine scoring is available and discusses such things as the grade level for which the test was designed, the cost of the test, the reliability and validity of the test, and the construction and standardization of the test. In addition, the reviews often discuss interpretative and other problems related to a particular test.

Section C-10 of the APGA *Ethical Standards* is consistent with the *Hobson* case discussed in this chapter. Both serve as a reminder that testing instruments may discriminate against minority groups unless such groups are represented in the norm group for standardization of a particular test. Otherwise, minority groups are compared to white, middle-class Americans who have different socioeconomic backgrounds and, in some cases, different language.

Counselors should be knowledgeable of their individual job responsibilities and limitations in testing; duties of psychologists, counselors, medical personnel and school administrators vary. In one study, for example, Talbutt (1979) reported that school psychologists, not guidance counselors, were responsible for tests given in the evaluation of students for special education. Guidance counselors, rather, serve as team members in classifying students. Although counseling duties vary among states, Talbutt found that school counselors could be responsible for interpreting test results for students, self-appraisal, conducting individual and group interpretation sessions for career development, using test results as a partial means of identifying students with special needs, and conducting individual and group interpretation sessions with parents. Training and skills of counselors vary. Yet all counselors are reminded that they must not go beyond their individual degree of competence and training. APGA *Ethical Standards* (1981), section C-4, addresses this issue: "Different tests demand different levels of competence for administration, scoring, and interpretation. Members must recognize the limits of their competence and perform only those functions for which they are prepared" (p. 2).

Public school counselors should follow all regulations and guidelines from their state and local boards of education. Likewise, professional counselors and psychologists licensed by state licensing boards should follow all ethical standards and regulations from the licensing organizations. Professional ethical standards provide excellent guidelines, but they address a national audience and do not reflect the various state regulations and specific state laws.

Further, counselors should keep up with current testing information in professional journals, conferences, and workshops. The APGA *Ethical Standards* (1981) recommends two articles: "The Responsible Use of Tests: A Position Paper of AMEG, APGA, and NCME" (1972) and "Responsibilities of Users of Standardized Tests" (1978).

CHAPTER GUIDELINES

1. Court rulings and laws stipulate that pupils should not be denied a free, public education because of sex, race, or handicaps. Once a state makes public education available, it should be available to all citizens equally.
2. Tests should be reliable as well as valid and should not result in the discrimination against individuals.
3. Tests have been misused in education. The instruments themselves have discriminated against certain groups, and the results have often been misinterpreted.
4. Test scores should not be used for ability grouping when that grouping discriminates against certain types of students.
5. The courts have indicated that test scores should not be the sole criterion for classifying and placing students.
6. No single test score should be used to classify persons. An error could lead to harmful results for the individual. Rather, classification should be based on a combination of data.
7. The courts have indicated that tests should be valid and relevant to the situation for which they are used. Tests should have a positive relationship with the program for which the scores are used. APGA *Ethical Standards* states that "the member must consider carefully the validity, reliability, and appropriateness of the test(s)" (1981).
8. Counselors have helpful ethical standards through professional groups on a range of issues including testing and placement. Both APGA *Ethical Standards* (1981) and "Ethical Principles of Psychologists" (1981) address the use of tests.

SITUATIONAL DISCUSSIONS

Situation 1: Think of an example appropriate for your work setting to illustrate a counselor's misuse of testing.

Situation 2: How have testing programs discriminated against certain students?

Situation 3: List recommendations for counselors that might help them avoid sex discrimination.

Situation 4: Identify some professional sources helpful to counselors regarding testing.

Situation 5: Define the counselor's role in testing for your work setting. Identify some potential danger areas that might lead to the misuse of tests.

REFERENCES

Bernard, M. L., and B. E. Gilliland, 1981, Sex bias in counseling: An examination of certain counselor characteristics and their effect on counseling behavior, *School Counselor* **29**(1):34-39.

Brolin, D. E., and N. C. Gysbers, 1979 (December), Career education for persons with handicaps, *Personnel and Guidance Journal,* pp. 258-262.

Buros, O. K., 1978, *Mental Measurements Yearbook,* 8th ed., Gryphon Press, Highland Park, N.J.

Ethical Principles of Psychologists, 1981, *American Psychologist* **36:**633-638.

Ethical Standards of the American Personnel and Guidance Association, 1981, Washington, D.C.

Harway, M., 1977, Sex bias in counseling materials, *Journal of College Personnel* **18:**57-63.

Hohenshil, T. H., and C. W. Humes, 1979 (December), Roles of counseling in ensuring the rights of the handicapped, *Personnel and Guidance Journal* **58:**221-227.

Kamin, L., 1975, Social and legal consequences of I.Q. tests as classification instruments: Some warnings from our past, *Journal of School Psychology* **13:**317-323.

Moore, H., and C. Strickler, 1980, The counseling profession's response to sex-biased counseling: An update, *Personnel and Guidance Journal* **59:**84-87.

McCarthy, M. M., and S. B. Thomas, 1977, The rights to an education: New trends emerging from special education litigation, *NOLPE School Law Journal* **7:**78-87.

Project on Equal Education Rights (PEER), 1975, *Summary of the Regulations for Title IX Education Ammendments of 1972,* Office for Civil Rights, U.S. Dept. HEW, Washington, D.C.

Pullin, D., 1981, Minimum competency testing and the demand for accountability, *Phi Delta Kappan* **63**(1):20-22.

Responsibilities of users of standardized tests, 1978 (October 5), *Guidepost,* pp. 5-8.

The responsible use of tests: A position paper of AMEG, APGA, and NCME, 1972, *Measurement and Evaluation in Guidance* **5:**385-388.

Ryland, W. H., 1975, Title IX regulations, in *Attorney General's Conference on School Law, Transcript of Proceedings,* Office of the Attorney General, Richmond, Va., pp. 46-57.

Shea, T. S., 1977, An educational perspective of the legality of intelligence testing and ability grouping, *Journal of Law and Education* **6:**137-158.

Standards for Educational and Psychological Testing, 1974, rev. ed., American Psychological Association, American Research Association, National Council on Measurement in Education, Washington, D.C.

Talbutt, L., 1979, Law and Virginia Public School Counselors, unpublished dissertation, Virginia Polytechnic Institute and State University.

Talbutt, L. C., 1983, The Counselor and testing: Some legal concerns, *School Counselor* **30:**245-250.

University of Pennsylvania, 1976, *University of Pennsylvania Law Review* **124**(3):806.

LEGAL REFERENCES

Brown v. Board of Education, 347 U.S. 483 (1954).

Copeland v. School Board of City of Portsmouth, 464F.2d 932 (E.D. Va. 1972).

Debra P. v. Turlington, 644 F.2d 397 (Fla. Cir. 1981).

Education for All Handicapped Children Act of 1975, Pub. L. No. 94-142 §3, 89 Stat. 773, 775-781 (1975); §4, 89 Stat. 775, 20 U.S.C. §1401 (1975); §612 89 Stat. 781, 20 U.S.C. §412 (1975).

Education Amendments of 1972, Pub. L. No. 92-318 §910, 86 Stat. 373, 235-375 (1972); 42 U.S.C. §2000.

Elementary and Secondary Education Amendments of 1974, Pub. L. No. 93-380, §202, 88 Stat. 514, 488-517 (1974); 20 U.S.C. §1701.

Griggs v. Duke Power Co., 401 U.S. 421 (1971).

Hobson v. Hansen, 269 F. Supp. 401 (D.C. Washington D.C. 1967).

Hoffman v. Board of Education, 410 N.Y.S.2d 99 (S.C. N.Y. 1978).

Mills v. Board of Education, 348 F. Supp. 866 (D.C. Washington D.C. 1972).

Moses v. Washington Parish School Board, 456 F.2d 1285 (E.D. La. 1972).

Pennsylvania Assn. for Retarded Children (P.A.R.C.) v. Commonwealth, 343 F. Supp. 279 (E.D. Pa. 1972).

Rehabilitation Act, Pub. L. No. 93-112, §503, 504 (1973).

Part III

ABORTION, DRUGS, AND CHILD ABUSE

Today counselors help clients with a range of personal problems. Van Hoose and Kottler (1978) wrote, "During the past decade the state has assumed increasing responsibility for such social problems as drug abuse, alcoholism, and crime and violence, and has relied heavily on counselors and psychotherapists as primary professionals in the treatment of these problems" (p. 14). They concluded that counseling services have expanded into all aspects of life. With counselors involved in many complex problems surrounded by ethical and legal issues, it is imperative that they become familiar with laws and court cases concerning a range of topics. As litigation changes, the counselor's role also changes. For example, the chapter on abortion illustrates legal changes within the past 10 years that have affected the counselor's role. Three areas of professional concern for counselors are covered in this section: abortion, drugs, and child abuse.

REFERENCE

Van Hoose, W. H., and J. Kottler, 1978, *Ethical and Legal Issues in Counseling and Psychotherapy,* Jossey-Bass, San Francisco.

Chapter 10

Abortion

The United States Supreme Court handed down several decisions regarding abortions in the 1970s. In 1973 the Supreme Court determined that women could terminate pregnancies for reasons other than to save their lives. Then in 1976 it ruled that it was unconstitutional for states to impose blanket parental permission for unmarried minors to obtain abortions. The law clearly allows abortions for both adults and minors. Even though the law is clear, the question often arises about the counselor's legal responsibility to the parents of minors. School counselors in particular struggle with their professional obligation to both parents and students.

CASES

A number of court cases, including Supreme Court decisions, have dealt with abortions. The United States Supreme Court in *Roe v. Wade* (1973) ruled that a Texas law that restricted legal abortions to those necessary to save a mother's life was in violation of the due process clause of the Fourteenth Amendment. For the first time in the United States, the Court determined that a woman had a privacy right regarding the termination of pregnancy.

Selected portions of this chapter are used with permission from L. C. Talbutt, 1983, Current legal trends regarding abortions for minors: A dilemma for counselors, *School Counselor* **31**(2): 120-124.

In *Doe v. Bolton* (1973), the United States Supreme Court declared that "three procedural conditions" of a Georgia statute were unconstitutional according to the Fourteenth Amendment (p. 180). The statute required hospital accreditation requirements, a review committee, consent by two copractitioners, and residency before a woman could obtain an abortion. This Court decision reduced the complexity of hospital requirements for abortions, making legal abortion more accessible to women.

A number of court cases have dealt with minors and abortions. The Supreme Court of Washington, in *State of Washington v. Koome* (1975), determined that a statute that required unmarried minors to have parental consent prior to abortion was an invasion of privacy rights and that it discriminated between types of women. "We hold that this statute too broadly encumbers the right of unmarried minor women to choose to terminate pregnancy, and unjustifiably discriminates between similarly situated groups of women in terms of their right to obtain a legal abortion" (p. 262).

In *Planned Parenthood v. Danforth* (1976), the United States Supreme Court ruled that a Missouri law that required consent by a parent in the case of an unmarried minor prior to an abortion was unconstitutional. Citing *Roe v. Wade* (1973), the Court concluded, "[T]he state may not constitutionally impose a blanket parental consent requirement" (p. 53).

More recently a Supreme Court ruling on abortion, *Bellotti v. Baird* (1979), struck down a Massachusetts statute that required minors to obtain parental consent prior to an abortion.

> We therefore conclude that if the State decides to require a pregnant minor to obtain one or both parents' consent to an abortion, it also must provide an alternative procedure whereby authorization for the abortion can be obtained. A pregnant minor is entitled in such a proceeding to show either: (1) that she is mature enough and well enough informed to make her abortion decision, in consultation with her physician, independently of her parents' wishes; or (2) that even if she is not able to make this decision independently, the desired abortion would be in her best interests.
>
> . . . In sum, the procedure must ensure that the provision requiring parental consent does not in fact amount to the "absolute, and possible arbitrary, veto" that was found impermissible in *Danforth*. (P. 4973)

Clearly, minors have the legal right to abortions according to the several Supreme Court cases cited. Parental permission may be required only if state statutes provide an alternative procedure whereby minors have opportunities to show they are mature enough to make the decision or that the abortion is in their best interest.

In *H. L. Etc. Appelant v. Scott M. Matheson* (1981), the Supreme Court upheld a Utah state law requiring doctors to notify parents of minors about abortions under certain conditions. The Court decided that a state may make the notification requirement if the girl is dependent on her parents, when she is not emancipated, and when she had made no claim that she is mature enough to make the decision alone or that her relationship with the parents might be seriously affected by such notification. Parental notification by physicians of a minor child's abortion was determined to be legal in certain circumstances.

More recently, in June 1983, the United States Supreme Court restated its position on abortion in three court decisions: *City of Akron v. Akron Center for Reproductive Health* (1983), *Planned Parenthood Assoc. of Kansas City, Mo., Inc. v. Ashcroft* (1983), and *Chris Simopaulas, Appellant v. Virginia* (1983). The Court decided that states may not require that all 2nd-trimester abortions be performed in a hospital, may not impose a 24-hour waiting period, may not require doctors to discuss the fetus as "a human life," and may not impose absolute parental consent for minors. Writing the majority opinion, Justice Powell "indicated that the meaning of the Constitution can't change every 10 years" ("The Court Stands by Abortion," 1983). Clearly, the United States Supreme Court reaffirmed that abortions are constitutional for women, both adults and minors.

THE COUNSELOR'S ROLE

Professional counselors in private practice probably face fewer conflicts in abortion counseling than do public school counselors. Counselors in private practice deal with clients who choose professional service, whereas school counselors serve minors who are legally required to attend school. The nature of counseling in the public school is different from counseling in other settings. Burgum and Anderson (1976) wrote that the school counselor serves three groups: students, parents, and society (p. 10). It is the conflict among these three groups that often creates confusion and legal problems for school counselors. Alexander (1976) maintained that the school counselor is in a "precarious ethical and legal position that must be balanced to ensure the counselees of their rights and to ensure the rights of others" (p. 227).

In defining the role of school counselor on abortion, Duncan and Moffett (1974) indicated a counselor should establish a setting in which clients examine the feelings and evaluate alternatives. They warned counselors against imposing their views and attitudes on clients (1974, 192). Walleat (1975) summarized the counselor's responsibilities into four areas. First of all, Walleat maintained abortion should be viewed in relationship to the student's total development rather than solely a crisis. Second, counselors should work in conjunction with other community and school programs. Third, counselors have a responsibility to help students "process" information. Finally, counselors should help students use information about abortion, even when schools fail to supply that information. Walleat emphasized that there may be possible legal and ethical issues regarding schools providing abortion information (p. 341). The extent to which schools can or should provide abortion information to minors is unclear. For example, do schools display information on abortion clinics openly? Is the information held discreetly for students requesting it? Can parents of minors legally object to schools disseminating information about abortion? Can the dissemination of information be interpreted as encouraging abortions?

Burgum and Anderson (1975) made some recommendations to help counselors avoid lawsuits regarding abortions. They suggested counselors give advice only in those areas in which they are competent according to their education and work experience. "Referring a counselee to a clinic's care is the wise, commonsense course for a counselor to follow" (p. 52). Referral is probably a good idea in public school settings where administrative policies and support for counselors are unclear. They also wrote that counselors who too "vociferously encourage abortion" (p. 193) or those who "negligently interfere with the parents' right to advise a minor" (p. 193-194) may face legal difficulties.

Ethical Standards of the American Personnel and Guidance Association (APGA) offers directions for counselors that may apply in abortion counseling.

> If the member determines an inability to be of professional assistance to the client, the member must either avoid initiating the counseling relationship or immediately terminate the relationship. In either event, the member must suggest appropriate alternatives. (The member must be knowledgeable about referral resources so that a satisfactory referral can be initiated.) In the event the client declines the suggested referral, the member is not obligated to continue the relationship. (*Ethical Standards,* 1981, 2)

This section of *Ethical Standards* is consistent with the earlier recommendation that counselors should not go beyond their skill and training. In abortion counseling, school counselors, or other professionals not qualified to handle serious psychological problems resulting from abortion, should make referrals to other professionals. Also, counselors should not answer medical questions related to abortions, or any other areas, beyond their training and skill. Those concerns should be referred to medical personnel.

CHAPTER GUIDELINES

1. In 1973 the United States Supreme Court determined that abortions were legal for reasons other than to save a woman's life.
2. The United States Supreme Court has determined that states may

require parental permission for minors to obtain abortions if alternative permission procedures are provided.

3. The United States Supreme Court has ruled that states may not require absolute or blanket parental permission for minors to obtain abortions.
4. The School Counselor serves society, clients, and the institution. Thus, the counselor functions in many conflicting situations between these three groups.
5. Counselors in private practice face fewer conflicts than the school counselor who works primarily with minors.
6. Counselors should be familiar with state laws and current court rulings that have legal implications for abortion counseling.
7. Counselors should be aware that they could face legal problems if they impose their views and attitudes on minors regarding abortions.
8. Counselors should note that they can face litigation if they go beyond their professional training skill in abortion counseling or in any other area of counseling. Serious medical and psychological problems should be left to medical and psychiatric personnel.
9. Counselors should urge minors to discuss abortion plans with parents and involve families in the counseling process if possible.
10. Counselors should work through their national, state, and local professional organizations for professional directions and guidelines on abortion counseling and dissemination of abortion information for minors in the school setting.

SITUATIONAL DISCUSSIONS

Situation 1: Abortions are clearly legal for both adults and minors. Identify some hypothetical situations in which counselors might go beyond their skill and training regarding abortion counseling.

Situation 2: Identify the counselor's role in abortion counseling. Is the school counselor's role more difficult than the role of other counselors? Why? Why not?

Situation 3: When the counselor has strong personal feelings about abortion and is unable to deal with a client objectively, what procedures would you recommend for the counselor? Identify sections within the APGA *Ethical Standards* that might provide guidelines for counselors.

REFERENCES

Alexander, D., 1976, Legal issues in guidance, in *School Guidance Services,* T. H. Hohenshil and J. H. Miles, eds., Kendal/Hunt, Dubuque, Iowa, pp. 219-246.

Burgum, T., and S. Anderson, 1975, *The Counselor and the Law,* APGA Press, Washington, D.C.

The Court stands by abortion, 1983 (June 27), *Newsweek,* pp. 62-63.

Duncan, J., and C. Moffett, 1974, Abortion counseling and the school counselor, *School Counselor* **21:**188-195.

Ethical Standards of the American Personnel and Guidance Association, 1981, Washington, D.C.

Walleat, P. L., 1975, Abortion information: A guidance viewpoint, *School Counselor* **22:**338-341.

LEGAL REFERENCES

Bellotti v. Baird, 47, LW 4969 (July 2, 1979).

Chris Simopoulas, Appelant v. Virginia, 51 LW 4791 (June 15, 1983).

City of Akron v. Akron Center for Reproductive Health, 51 LW, 4767 (June 15, 1983).

Doe v. Bolton, 410, U.S. 179 (1973).

H. L. Etc., Appelant v. Scott M. Matheson, 101 S.Ct. 1164 (1981).

Planned Parenthood Assn. of Kansas City, Mo., Inc. v. Ashcroft, 51 LW, 4783 (June 15, 1983).

Planned Parenthood v. Danforth, 428 U.S. 52 (1976).

Roe v. Wade, 410 U.S. 113 (1973).

State of Washington v. Koome, 530 P.2d 260 (S.C. Wash. 1975).

Chapter 11

Drugs

As drug abuse increases, counselors must focus on the problems created for the client and others resulting from drugs. This chapter does not address counseling techniques but focuses on some legal issues pertaining to drug abuse. The issues are more complex for school counselors then for counselors in other settings. First, school counselors have responsibilities both to the client and to other students. Alexander (1976) explained that there are times when the counselor as "an arm of the administration" must put the welfare of other students over that of the counselee (p. 227). Second, drugs in school may lead to illegal search and seizure. Burgum and Anderson (1975) identified illegal search as one potential area for liability against counselors. They emphasized that to use counselors to participate in search and seizure is a "misuse of a counselor's specialty" (p. 56). In fact, it is generally agreed upon that major disciplinary problems should be handled by administrators, not counselors. Nevertheless, counselors and other school personnel should have some familiarity with search and seizure policies and litigation in the event that they are drawn into search and seizure or have indirect association

---

Selected portions of this chapter are used with permission from L. C. Talbutt, 1980, Medical rights of minors: Some answered and unanswered questions, *School Counselor* **27**:403-406 and L. C. Talbutt, 1983, Recent court decisions: A quiz for APGA members, *Personnel and Guidance Journal* **61**:355-357.

with such a procedure. Counselor involvement in search and seizure is not recommended.

Regarding the use of illegal drugs, Nolte (1977) wrote, "It is a concern school counselors probably face more wrenchingly than any other segment of a given school building staff" (p. 44). Nolte also reported that minors in some states may receive treatment for drug addiction without parental consent. Regardless of their work setting, counselors should know their state's law regarding the rights of minors for medical/drug treatment. For example, in Virginia, minors may consent to medical or health services needed in the case of outpatient care, treatment, or rehabilitation for substance abuse without parental permission. (*Virginia Code,* 1979). State laws vary, so it is imperative that counselors check the exact wording of their particular state law.

Counselors and educators have been warned against labeling students as potential drug abusers. In *Merriken v. Cressman* (1973), the Pennsylvania Eastern District Court ruled that a drug prevention program violated the privacy rights of the family. In that case the tests contained personal questions used to determine potential drug abusers. Also, two psychiatrists testified that the drug program could have the effects of a "self-fulfilling prophecy" in which children labeled as a potential drug abuser could decide to become what they had been labeled. Children so labeled might receive "unpleasant" treatment from their peers (p. 915). The court offered the following explanation: "When a program talks about labeling someone as a particular type and such a label could remain with him for the remainder of his life, the margin of error must be almost nil. The preliminary statistics and other evidence indicate there will be errors in identification" (p. 920).

The American School Counselor Association's "Position Statement" (1976) recommended that school counselors make referrals when appropriate in drug counseling. "Referral to appropriate agencies and/or other professional consultation is an integral part of the counselor's responsibility." (p. 284).

Regarding the courts' position on search and seizure in public schools, Connelly (1982), noted in summary that courts have upheld searches when school personnel have acted within "the scope of their job" to maintain discipline for the health and safety of students and when searches have been based on "concrete, articulable facts" (p. 155). However, Connelly pointed out that "random, causeless searches will not be upheld by the courts" (p. 155). In situations in which administrators were acting on "*a hunch or mere suspicion,*" Connelly wrote, "the courts did not uphold the search" (p. 146). Connelly further explained that the courts will consider how the search was conducted and the purpose of the search (p. 230).

A fairly recent development pertaining to drug searches in schools is the use of dogs to sniff out narcotics. In *Diane Doe v. Omar Renfrow* (1979), with certiorari denied by the United States Supreme Court on May 26, 1981, the Court determined that dogs trained to sniff out narcotics did not constitute an unreasonable search in the school; but the Court ruled that "strip" or nude searches resulting from a dog's alert can be unconstitutional if students do not have a previous history of drug use. Thus, school administrators should be extremely careful in using dogs for drug searches. The Court also determined that requiring students to empty their pockets was not a violation of student rights. However, the court offered the following warning to school administrators regarding nude searches:

> Subjecting a student to a nude search is more than just the mild inconvenience of a pocket search, rather, it is an intrusion into an individual's basic justifiable expectation of privacy. Before such a search can be performed, the school administrators must articulate some fact that provides a reasonable cause to believe the student possesses the contraband sought. (*Diane Doe,* 1979, 1024)

Then in *Jones v. Latexo Independent School District* (1980), dogs were used to inspect both students and the parking lot. In comparing the use of dogs to electronic surveillance equipment, the court ruled that the search was unreasonable. In this particular situation, the students were informed about the search in assembly with each student being inspected by the trained dogs. The search was not based on facts or reasonable suspicion.

CHAPTER GUIDELINES

1. Counselors should make every effort to avoid handling disciplinary problems such as search and seizure. These areas of discipline come under administrators' responsibilities. Counselors may be called upon to explain policies and procedures. In such instances, a brief explanation of search and seizure is helpful.
2. Counselors should be familiar with state laws regarding the rights of minors to drug treatment. Some states allow minors treatment without parental permission.
3. Counselors are warned against labeling potential drug users because there are no testing instruments that are error free. Also, such labeling could have a self-fulfilling prophecy.
4. Counselors should make appropriate referrals in drug counseling. As in other areas, counselors should refer clients when an area is beyond their skill and training.
5. The courts have determined that school personnel may conduct searches in schools if there is reasonable cause or if the search comes

under the administrator's role in maintaining health and safety standards for students. Searches without cause or good reason have not been upheld by the courts.

6. One court case indicated that dogs may be used to search for drugs in schools; however, strip or nude searches resulting from sniffer dogs' findings were not upheld, especially when the search was not based upon facts or reasonable cause. Another court ruling determined that a blanket or general search was unconstitutional. Until more court decisions are made, administrators should proceed carefully.
7. Because canine searches are relatively recent occurrences, counselors should keep up with new rulings to determine the court's direction regarding this aspect of search and seizure.

SITUATIONAL DISCUSSIONS

Situation 1: Search and seizure is not the responsibility of counselors. Identify some ways in which school counselors might be drawn into such procedures. How might school counselors prevent involvement in search and seizure?

Situation 2: Besides legal difficulties, identify disadvantages of using dogs in school searches. In your opinion, would the use of dogs ever be justified? Explain.

REFERENCES

Alexander, D., 1976, Legal issues in guidance, in *School Guidance Services,* T. H. Hohenshil and J. H. Miles, eds., Kendal/Hunt, Dubuque, Iowa, pp. 219-246.

American School Counselor Association, 1976, Position statements, *School Counselor* **323:**281-288.

Burgum, T., and S. Anderson, 1975, *The Counselor and the Law,* APGA Press, Washington, D.C.

Connelly, M. J., 1982, Search and Seizure in Education, unpublished dissertation, Virginia Polytechnic Institute and State University.

Nolte, M. C., 1982, How to keep your guidance counselor out of court, *American School Board Journal* **164:**44-45.

LEGAL REFERENCES

Diane Doe v. Omar Renfrow et al., 475 F. Supp. 1012 (N.D. Ind. 1979).

Jones v. Latexo Independent School District, 499 F. Supp. 223 (E.D. Tex. 1980).

Merriken v. Cressman, 364 F. Supp. 913 (E.D. Pa. 1973).

Virginia Code Ann. § § 54-325.2 (1979).

Chapter 12

Child Abuse

Child abuse continues to be a serious problem in the United States. Shanas (1975) wrote, "Some ten thousand children are severely battered each year; 50,000 to 75,000 are sexually abused; 100,000 are 'emotionally neglected'; and another 100,000 are physically, morally, or educationally neglected" (p. 479). Shanas reported that the first documented case of child abuse occurred in New York City over a century ago. However, Shanas concluded that it has only been within the last 10 years that the problem has received national attention.

Miles (1980, 47) reported that "child abuse continues to occur at an alarming rate in today's society." Miles reported three fundamental barriers in our society that allow child abuse and neglect to go unchecked.

> The first is a tradition of family autonomy—the family's right to privacy and the unwritten belief that parents know what they are doing in raising children. Secondly, there exists a healthy acceptance of physical force as a valid means of resolving conflict, even when the conflict involves children. The old adage, *Spare the rod—spoil the child,* is alive and flourishing. Thirdly, there is some confusion about where appropriate corporal punishment ends and child abuse begins. (P. 47)

Selected portions of this chapter are used with permission from L. C. Talbutt, 1981, Child abuse: A team approach for elementary counselors, *Elementary School Guidance and Counseling* **16**(2):142-145.

Child abuse is a problem not only for school counselors. This chapter makes several references to school counselors' responsibility because they work with minors and children. However, the following two court cases illustrate that physicians and psychiatrists may also face litigation for failure to report child abuse. Clearly counselors and others in the helping professions have an ethical responsibility to report child abuse and a legal duty when mandated by law.

In *Landeros v. Flood* (1976), the Supreme Court of California, in reversing a lower court decision, determined that a physician and hospital could be liable for a child's injuries if they "negligently failed to diagnose and report battered child syndrome, resulting in the child's being returned to her parents and receivng further injuries at their hands" (p. 389).

Then, in 1980 a Florida court of appeals in *Groff v. State of Florida* (1980) reviewed and denied a rehearing of a case concerning a psychiatrist who failed to report child abuse. That case revealed that Florida law effective October 1, 1977, on child abuse did not set forth a penalty for failure to report. Florida law in 1975 did have such a penalty. The psychiatrist in question was charged for failure to report between March 1, 1977 and March 31, 1978. In the final decision, the court pointed out that Dr. Groff was subject to penalty for failure to report child abuse prior to October 1, 1977; but according to Florida statute (1977) he was not subject to a penalty after the new statute was effective. Although legal technicalities make this case difficult for the lay reader of law, counselors should know that a footnote in the case revealed that the Florida statute "was amended in 1979 to provide a penalty for circumstances such as exist in this case" (p. 362). Clearly, child abuse and child-abuse reporting should be concerns for school counselors, psychologists, psychiatrists, and others in the helping professions.

LEGAL RAMIFICATIONS FOR COUNSELORS

In 1974 the Child Abuse Prevention and Treatment Act, Public Law 93-247 was passed to provide financial help "for the prevention, identification, and treatment of child abuse and neglect and establish a National Center on child abuse and neglect" (88 Stat. 4). The law gives the following definition of child abuse: "Sec. 3 For purposes of this Act the term "child abuse and neglect" means the physical or mental injury, sexual abuse, negligent treatment, or maltreatment of a child under the age of eighteen by a person who is responsible for the child's welfare" (88 Stat. 5).

In addition to Public Law 93-247, all states have new legislation regarding the reporting of child abuse (Grigg and Gale, 1977). Details of state laws vary.

Cambin and Prout (1983) reported the results of a study concerning all states and the District of Columbia. Not only did they find that all states have mandatory reporting laws for child abuse, but they found that all states and the District of Columbia grant immunity from civil or criminal liability for individuals reporting in good faith (p. 360). This simply means a person who makes an error in reporting child abuse is not liable unless malicious intent can be shown. Cambin and Prout (1983) also reported that all states require school personnel to report suspected cases of child abuse with 46 states naming "counselor" as a mandatory reporter. Cashey and Richardson (1975) found that state laws varied according to the professionals required to report child abuse. For example, they found 22 states requiring social workers to report child abuse, some states naming teachers separately and some states grouping school authorities together (p. 198).

Failure to report child abuse has legal ramifications for counselors, social workers, teachers and others involved in the helping professions. Teachers in New York City, for example, who fail to report child abuse may be found guilty of a misdemeanor and civil liability damages (Shanas, 1975, 480). In another example, Virginia law requires certain professionals to report child abuse and establishes that failure to do so can result in a fine. The law also grants immunity from civil and criminal liability to those persons required to report child abuse. Therefore, an honest error in judgment would not result in litigation against the reporter unless the person making the report had acted with malicious intent. The following citation illustrates one state law concerning child abuse.

> A. . . . [A]ny teacher or other person employed in a public or private school, kindergarten or nursery school, any person providing full- or part-time child care for pay on a regularly planned basis . . . who has reason to suspect that a child is an abused or neglected child, shall report the matter immediately, except as hereinafter provided, to the local department of the county or city wherein the child resides or wherein the abuse or neglect is believed to have occurred . . . . B. Any person required to file a report pursuant to sub-section A of this section who is found guilty . . . shall be fined not more than five hundred dollars for the first failure and for any subsequent failures not less than one hundred dollars nor more than one thousand dollars. (*Virginia Code,* 1975)

This particular state law also grants immunity from liability to any person reporting child abuse. "Any person making a report . . . , or who takes a child into custody . . . , or who participates in a judicial proceeding resulting therefrom shall be immune from any civil or criminal liability therewith, unless it is proven that such person acted with malicious intent" (*Virginia Code,* 1975).

Counselors should be familiar with the exact wording of the child abuse laws in their individual states. Because state laws vary, counselors should be aware of the professionals named in the law, specified procedures for reporting, immunity rights, and other details. The following section will provide some specific recommendations and procedures helpful to counselors.

RECOMMENDATIONS FOR COUNSELORS

Counselors, psychologists and others in the helping professions have a major responsibility to report child abuse. First, counselors must be able to recognize child abuse and neglect (Grigg and Gale, 1977, 192). Schmitt (1975) described child abuse and neglect "as any condition injurious to the child's physical or emotional health that has been inflicted by parents, guardians, or other caretakers" (p. 58). Grigg and Gale (1977) gave "underweight," "anemia," "bruises," "welts," and "broken bones" as clues that indicate abuse and suggested the school nurse could be of aid to the school counselor. In addition, abused children display certain behavioral characteristics. The authors wrote, "These range from silence, withdrawal, fear, and submissiveness to anger, hostility, and aggression" (p. 192). They summarized the counselor's role in the following way: "The counselor needs to be in the forefront of child advocacy, intervening on behalf of children . . . The counselor plays a vital role in conjunction with other persons in the medical and helping profession in the identification, referral and treatment of abused youth" (Grigg and Gale, 1977, p. 194).

All helping professionals have a moral and ethical duty to report child abuse. Many professionals, including school personnel, counselors, social workers, psychologists, medical personnel and others, are legally bound by state laws to report child abuse. Because of their work setting, school counselors and teachers, more than any other professional group, have the greatest opportunity to be exposed to large numbers of children suffering from child abuse. A section from the American School Counselor Association "Position Statements" (1983, 1-2) on child abuse (adapted January 1981) provides some clear guidelines for counselors regarding what and how to report child abuse:

> School counselors who suspect a child is being abused or neglected should report the following information to the appropriate authority as soon as possible:
>
> 1. Name and address of the child and parent (or guardian).
> 2. Child's sex.
> 3. Nature and extent of the child's injuries, abuse or neglect.
> 4. Any evidence of prior injuries, abuse or neglect.
> 5. Action, if any, taken to treat, shelter or assist the child.
> 6. Name of the person or persons making the report.

7. Other pertinent information. . . .

The following sample procedures may be used in referring suspected child abuse/neglect:

1. Any school counselor who suspects that a child has been abused shall report this as soon as possible to the principal (designee) on the day of observation.
2. The principal (designee) will review the report and school information with appropriate staff members within two days of the referral; reasonable cause must be determined before informing the appropriate referral agency.
3. The school principal or designee shall call the appropriate referral agency (telephone number) and notify them of the alleged child abuse.
   a. You may request that the agency case worker maintain contact with a specific school staff member.
   b. You may ask that the specific identity of the reporter remain confidential (instead, the referral agency, if asked, would state that the referral came from the ______________________ School Department).
4. Within two working days, the school principal or designee shall submit a written report to the appropriate agency. This confidential report may be sent by registered mail. A photostatic copy of this confidential report may be forwarded to the Superintendent of Schools or designee.
5. If the appropriate agency does not respond to your report within 60 days, you are to refile the report. However, if no response, contact will be made within 20 days of the original notification.

Forrer (1975) made some specific recommendations for school counselors dealing with child abuse. He advised counselors to maintain established procedures that included referral, medical, and legal reporting information. Forrer also suggested that counselors learn about their particular state law on child abuse through their state attorney general's office. Additionally, he believed that counselors should become knowledgeable about child abuse and educate other school personnel. Lastly, Forrer suggested that counselors participate in planning curriculum dealing with parenting, child care, and the family in order to reduce future problems in child abuse (1975, 165). Talbutt (1981) summarized two ways public school counselors can effectively intervene in child abuse. One, the counselor should become acquainted with the symptoms of child abuse and should work on a team with teachers, school nurses, and others to recognize and deal with child abuse. Two, counselors should take the lead in organizing workshops and programs in the prevention and treatment of child abuse (p. 143).

CHAPTER GUIDELINES

1. Child abuse continues to be a serious problem in the United States. Counselors and others in the helping professions should be advocates of the rights of children.

2. State laws dealing with child abuse vary; thus, professionals should be familiar with the exact wording of child abuse laws for their states.
3. The failure of counselors, psychologists, and other professionals to report child abuse can result in litigation and a fine against the professional.
4. Counselors, psychologists, and other helping professionals should participate actively in the recognition, treatment, and prevention of child abuse.
5. Counselors should report suspected cases of child abuse, act in good faith, and keep the reporting free from malicious intent.
6. Counselors have an ethical duty to report child abuse and a legal duty when the law mandates reporting. Counselors do not have to prove or investigate child abuse. Generally, their duty is to report child abuse to the agency responsible for investigating and dealing with child abuse.

SITUATIONAL DISCUSSIONS

Situation 1: Counselors have a legal and ethical duty to report child abuse. When might reporting child abuse lead to legal difficulties for counselors?

Situation 2: Identify some established procedures that would help counselors deal with child abuse counseling and reporting.

Situation 3: Child abuse prevention is important for future generations. What can educators do to help students better understand and prevent child abuse? Be specific.

Situation 4: The team approach is recommended for school professionals dealing with child abuse. Why is the team approach recommended? What are some advantages of this approach?

REFERENCES

American School Counselor Association, 1983, Position statements, *School Counselor* **20:**1-8.

Cambin, L. D., and H. T. Prout, 1983, School counselors and the reporting of child abuse: A survey of state laws and practices, *School Counselor* **30:**358-367.

Cashey, O. L., and I. Richardson, 1975, Understanding and helping child-abusing parents, *Elementary School Guidance and Counseling* **9:**196-208.

Forrer, S. E., 1975, Battered children and counselor responsibility, *School Counselor* **22:**161-165.

Grigg, S. A., and P. Gale, 1977, The abused child: Focus for counselors, *Elementary School Guidance and Counseling* **11:**187-194.

Miles, J. H., 1980, Child abuse and neglect: The counselor and the law, *Virginia Personnel and Guidance Journal* **8**(1):47-52.

Schmitt, B. D., 1975, What teachers need to know about child abuse and neglect, *Childhood Education* **52:**58-62.

Shanas, B., 1975, Child abuse: A killer teachers can help control, *Phi Delta Kappan* **56:**479-482.

Talbutt, L. C., 1981, Child abuse: A team approach for elementary counselors, *Elementary School Guidance and Counseling* **16**(2):142-145.

LEGAL REFERENCES

Child Abuse Prevention and Treatment Act, Pub. L. No. 93-247, §3, 88 Stat. 4, 4-5 (1974).

Groff v. State of Florida, 390 S.2d 368, (2nd D.C. Fla. 1980).

Landeros v. Flood, 551 P.2d 389 (S.C. Calif. 1976)

Virginia Code Ann. §63.1-248.3 (1975).

Virginia Code Ann. §54-325.2 (1978).

Appendix A

Legal Research

Legal research is the process of using certain procedures to locate primary and secondary legal sources. Cohen (1976) defined legal research as methodology and techniques for using published sources of the law (p. xv). Roalfe (1965) believed that legal research is "the functional counterpart of legal bibliography." Legal bibliography was defined as "published sources and materials of the law." Roalfe (1965) described *three distinct steps in legal research.* The procedure includes: (1) identifying sources pertinent to the research question; (2) expanding the search to include all of the information; and (3) updating the search (pp. 5-6).

Beyond these steps, Roalfe (1965, 6) suggested that collected data be categorized according to an organized system: that a separate record be maintained for each source on uniform paper with the complete citation. The method allows the researcher flexibility in organizing the sources.

In a discussion of the procedural steps, Roalfe described step one as the means for locating a specific book or exact page number of a court case or statute. Analyzing the issue "boils down, then, in most cases, simply to picking out all the concrete words, finding their synonyms . . . and trying them out on an index" (p. 21). Step two is described as an expansion of step one. The researcher follows the findings of step one to collect the needed information. Step three, described as being of "paramount importance," allows the researcher to determine if any recent changes have occurred in the statute or court decision. Shepard's citations system provides a history of reported cases that explains what has happened to a case on appeal and lists opinions about the case. Likewise, the system provides a history of statutory laws that explains whether legislation has been "amended, repealed, re-enacted, revised or superseded . . . or found to be constitutional, unconstitutional, valid, invalid or void by court action" (Roalfe, 1965, 221).

MATERIALS

Legal research utilizes search books to locate primary and secondary sources dealing with the law. Published sources of the law (legal bibliography) mentioned by Cohen in the definition of legal research are divided into three classifications: "(a) primary sources; (b) search books or finding-tools; and (c) secondary materials" (Cohen, 1971, 1).

Primary Sources

Under primary sources Cohen included statutes, court decisions, rulings and regulations by administrative agencies, and executive orders. The authors of this book have used the following primary sources related to counseling: court decisions, statutes, policies and regulations, and opinions by attorney generals.

Search Books

Cohen (1979, 4) described search books as the means by which the primary sources are located. Such materials as digests, encyclopedias, and phrase-books are included in this category. The *American Digest System, Corpus Juris Secundum, American Jurisprudence,* and the *American Law Reports, Annotated* are specific examples of search books.

Search for Court Cases. A major search tool for case law is the *American Digest System.* Cohen (1979) reported that the West Publishing Company has the most complete digest for case law. The *American Digest System* covers substantively all American appellate cases since 1658. The system is divided into nine segments according to dates.

Cases published in the *National Reporter System* are arranged by appropriate topics in the digest system. Thus, by a cross reference system, the researcher may locate a desired case by topic in the *American Digest System* and be referred to the case reported in its entirety in the *National Reporter System.*

The *National Reporter System* is divided into nine publications according to geographical location. For example, the *Southeastern Reporter* covers one geographical location that includes Virginia, West Virginia, North Carolina, South Carolina, and Georgia. Supreme Court cases and federal and state appellate cases are also made available by West Publishing Company.

Cohen (1976) gave three research methods for using the *West Digest System:* "the fact or descriptive word approach, the topical approach, and the case method" (p. 63). In the first approach, a researcher can select words that fit the research question, use the *Descriptive Word Index,* and locate other cases described by similar words. The topic approach is useful when the researcher knows the topic of his research question. Topics are listed in the front of each volume, and the searcher simply needs to turn to the desired topic. The case method allows the researcher to locate the citation for a case when the correct name of the case is known.

The legal encyclopedias *Corpus Juris Secundum* and *American Jurisprudence* are useful in locating citations. Each records legal topics alphabetically. Roalfe (1965, 23) explained that the topics are discussed at the top of the page and are secondary sources; however, the citations at the bottom of the page lead to primary sources. In addition, *American Law Reports, Annotated* is a useful tool. It is a digest of cases, similar to the *American Digest System,* and provides "subject access . . . by indexes and digests" (Cohen, 1971, 55).

Search for State Statutes, Agency Regulations, and Opinions by the State Attorneys General. Statutes are published by states on a regular basis, and the state departments of education often publish the laws of their states about education. Rezny (1968, 1-2) observed that statutes are "a better research tool because the state departments' publications may appear infrequently, and the laws may be numbered differently from the state codes." Roalfe (1965, 128) reported that revisions of state laws, generally called codes, are kept current by added pockets in the back of the book.

Cohen (1971, 245) and Roalfe (1965, 167-169) mentioned materials from state administrative departments as materials of value in legal research. Cohen reported that "publication of regulations is left to the descretion of the particular agency" and may be infrequent (p. 245).

Both Cohen (1971, 246) and Roalfe (1965, 271) believed that opinions by the attorneys general of the states are valuable in legal research. However, they explained that the opinions are advisory statements and interpretations of the law. Thus, they fall somewhere between primary and secondary sources. Each state publishes opinions by its attorney general.

Secondary Sources

Cohen's (1971) third category of materials was secondary sources. This classification included "textbooks, treatises, commentaries, restatements and periodicals which explain and describe the law" (p. 4). The *Index to Legal Periodicals* and the *Index to Periodical Articles Related to Law* are examples of tools that can be used to locate secondary sources for legal research.

SUMMARY

Legal research is a methodology in which specific use is made of legal search books to locate primary and secondary sources of the law. This methodology allows the researcher to identify sources related to the issue, expand the search to include all materials, and update the search. Primary sources includes court cases, statutes, regulations, and opinions by the state attorneys general.

REFERENCES

Cohen, M. L., 1971, *Legal Research in a Nutshell,* West, St. Paul, Minn.

Cohen, M. L., ed., 1976, *How to Find the Law,* 7th ed., West, St. Paul, Minn.

Rezny, A. A., 1968, *A Schoolman in the Law Library,* 2nd ed., The Interstate Printers and Publishers, Danville, Ill.

Roalfe, W. R., ed., 1965, *How to Find the Law,* 6th ed., West, St. Paul, Minn.

Appendix B

Ethical Standards of the American Personnel and Guidance Association

(Approved by Executive Committee upon referral of the Board of Directors, January 17, 1981).

Preamble

The American Personnel and Guidance Association is an educational, scientific, and professional organization whose members are dedicated to the enhancement of the worth, dignity, potential, and uniqueness of each individual and thus to the service of society.

The Association recognizes that the role definitions and work settings of its members include a wide variety of academic disciplines, levels of academic preparation and agency services. This diversity reflects the breadth of the Association's interest and influence. It also poses challenging complexities in efforts to set standards for the performance of members, desired requisite preparation or practice, and supporting social, legal, and ethical controls.

The specification of ethical standards enables the Association to clarify to present and future members and to those served by members, the nature of ethical responsibilities held in common by its members.

The existence of such standards serves to stimulate greater concern by members for their own professional functioning and for the conduct of fellow professionals such as counselors, guidance and student personnel workers, and others in the helping professions. As the ethical code of the Association,

---

Reprinted from pages 401-411 of Pupil Services: Development, Coordination, Administration, by Dean L. Hummel and Charles W. Humes, Macmillan Publishing Company, New York and Collier Macmillan Publishers, London, 1984, 480p., by permission of the publisher and of the American Personnel and Guidance Association; copyright © 1981 by the American Personnel and Guidance Association.

this document establishes principles that define the ethical behavior of Association members.

Section A—General

1. The member influences the development of the profession by continuous efforts to improve professional practices, teaching, services, and research. Professional growth is continuous throughout the member's career and is exemplified by the development of a philosophy that explains why and how a member functions in the helping relationship. Members must gather data on their effectiveness and be guided by the findings.

2. The member has a responsibility both to the individual who is served and to the institution within which the service is performed to maintain high standards of professional conduct. The member strives to maintain the highest levels of professional services offered to the individuals to be served. The member also strives to assist the agency, organization, or institution in providing the highest caliber of professional services. The acceptance of employment in an institution implies that the member is in agreement with the general policies and principles of the institution. Therefore the professional activities of the member are also in accord with the objectives of the institution. If, despite concerted efforts, the member cannot reach agreement with the employer as to acceptable standards of conduct that allow for changes in institutional policy conducive to the positive growth and development of clients, then terminating the affiliation should be seriously considered.

3. Ethical behavior among professional associates, both members and nonmembers, must be expected at all times. When information is possessed that raises doubt as to the ethical behavior of professional colleagues, whether Association members or not, the member must take action to attempt to rectify such a condition. Such action shall use the institution's channels first and then use procedures established by the state Branch, Division, or Association.

4. The member neither claims nor implies professional qualifications exceeding those possessed and is responsible for correcting any misrepresentations of these qualifications by others.

5. In establishing fees for professional counseling services, members must consider the financial status of clients and locality. In the event that the established fee structure is inappropriate for a client, assistance must be provided in finding comparable services of acceptable cost.

6. When members provide information to the public or to subordinates, peers or supervisors, they have a responsibility to ensure that the content is general, unidentified client information that is accurate, unbiased, and consists of objective, factual data.

7. With regard to the delivery of professional services, members should accept only those positions for which they are professionally qualified.

8. In the counseling relationship the counselor is aware of the intimacy of

the relationship and maintains respect for the client and avoids engaging in activities that seek to meet the counselor's personal needs at the expense of that client. Through awareness of the negative impact of both racial and sexual stereotyping and discrimination, the counselor guards the individual rights and personal dignity of the client in the counseling relationship.

Section B—Counseling Relationship

This section refers to practices and procedures of individual and/or group counseling relationships.

The member must recognize the need for client freedom of choice. Under those circumstances where this is not possible, the member must apprise clients of restrictions that may limit their freedom of choice.

1. The member's *primary* obligation is to respect the integrity and promote the welfare of the client(s), whether the client(s) is (are) assisted individually or in a group relationship. In a group setting, the member is also responsible for taking reasonable precautions to protect individuals from physical and/or psychological trauma resulting from interaction within the group.

2. The counseling relationship and information resulting therefrom be kept confidential, consistent with the obligations of the member as a professional person. In a group counseling setting, the counselor must set a norm of confidentiality regarding all group participants' disclosures.

3. If an individual is already in a counseling relationship with another professional person, the member does not enter into a counseling relationship without first contacting and receiving the approval of that other professional. If the member discovers that the client is in another counseling relationship after the counseling relationship begins, the member must gain the consent of the other professional or terminate the relationship, unless the client elects to terminate the other relationship.

4. When the client's condition indicates that there is clear and imminent danger to the client or others, the member must take reasonable personal action or inform responsible authorities. Consultation with other professionals must be used where possible. The assumption of responsibility for the client(s) behavior must be taken only after careful deliberation. The client must be involved in the resumption of responsibility as quickly as possible.

5. Records of the counseling relationship, including interview notes, test data, correspondence, tape recordings, and other documents, are to be considered professional information for use in counseling and they should not be considered a part of the records of the institution or agency in which the counselor is employed unless specified by state statute or regulation. Revelation to others of counseling material must occur only upon the expressed consent of the client.

6. Use of data derived from a counseling relationship for purposes of counselor training or research shall be confined to content that can be disguised to ensure full protection of the identity of the subject client.

7. The member must inform the client of the purposes, goals, techniques, rules of procedure and limitations that may affect the relationship at or before the time that the counseling relationship is entered.

8. The member must screen prospective group participants, especially when the emphasis is on self-understanding and growth through self-disclosure. The member must maintain an awareness of the group participants' compatibility throughout the life of the group.

9. The member may choose to consult with any other professionally competent person about a client. In choosing a consultant, the member must avoid placing the consultant in a conflict of interest situation that would preclude the consultant's being a proper party to the member's efforts to help the client.

10. If the member determines an inability to be of professional assistance to the client, the member must either avoid initiating the counseling relationship or immediately terminate that relationship. In either event, the member must suggest appropriate alternatives. (The member must be knowledgeable about referral resources so that a satisfactory referral can be imitated). In the event the client declines the suggested referral, the member is not obligated to continue the relationship.

11. When the member has other relationships, particularly of an administrative, supervisory and/or evaluative nature with an individual seeking counseling services, the member must not serve as the counselor but should refer the individual to another professional. Only in instances where such an alternative is unavailable and where the individual's situation warrants counseling intervention should the member enter into and/or maintain a counseling relationship. Dual relationships with clients that might impair the member's objectivity and professional judgment (e.g., as with close friends or relatives, sexual intimacies with any client) must be avoided and/or the counseling relationship terminated through referral to another competent professional.

12. All experimental methods of treatment must be clearly indicated to prospective recipients and safety precautions are to be adhered to by the member.

13. When the member is engaged in short-term group treatment/training programs (e.g., marathons and other encounter-type or growth groups), the member ensures that there is professional assistance available during and following the group experience.

14. Should the member be engaged in a work setting that calls for any variation from the above statements, the member is obligated to consult with other professionals whenever possible to consider justifiable alternatives.

Section C—Measurement and Evaluation

The primary purpose of educational and psychological testing is to provide descriptive measures that are objective and interpretable in either comparative or absolute terms. The member must recognize the need to interpret the statements that follow as applying to the whole range of appraisal techniques including test and nontest data. Test results constitute only one of a variety of pertinent sources of information for personnel, guidance, and counseling decisions.

1. The member must provide specific orientation or information to the examinee(s) prior to and following the test administration so that the results of testing may be placed in proper perspective with other relevant factors. In so doing, the member must recognize the effects of socioeconomic, ethnic and cultural factors on test scores. It is the member's professional responsibility to use additional unvalidated information carefully in modifying interpretation of the test results.

2. In selecting tests for use in a given situation or with a particular client, the member must consider carefully the specific validity, reliability, and appropriateness of the test(s). *General* validity, reliability and the like may be questioned legally as well as ethically when tests are used for vocational and educational selection, placement, or counseling.

3. When making any statements to the public about tests and testing, the member must give accurate information and avoid false claims or misconceptions. Special efforts are often required to avoid unwarranted connotations of such terms as *IQ* and *grade equivalent scores.*

4. Different tests demand different levels of competence for administration, scoring, and interpretation. Members must recognize the limits of their competence and perform only those functions for which they are prepared.

5. Tests must be administered under the same conditions that were established in their standardization. When tests are not administered under standard conditions or when unusual behavior or irregularities occur during the testing session, those conditions must be noted and the results designated as invalid or of questionable validity. Unsupervised or inadequately supervised test-taking, such as the use of tests through the mails, is considered unethical. On the other hand, the use of instruments that are so designed or standardized to be self-administered and self-scored, such as interest inventories, is to be encouraged.

6. The meaningfulness of tests results used in personnel, guidance, and counseling functions generally depends on the examinee's unfamiliarity with the specific items on the test. Any prior coaching or dissemination of the test materials can invalidate test results. Therefore, test security is one of the professional obligations of the member. Conditions that produce most favorable test results must be made known to the examinee.

7. The purpose of testing and the explicit use of the results must be made known to the examinee prior to testing. The counselor must ensure that instrument limitations are not exceeded and that periodic review and/or retesting are made to prevent client stereotyping.

8. The examinee's welfare and explicit prior understanding must be the criteria for determining the recipients of the test results. The member must see that specific interpretation accompanies any release of individual or group

test data. The interpretation of test data must be related to the examinee's particular concerns.

9. The member must be cautious when interpreting the results of research instruments possessing insufficient technical data. The specific purposes for the use of such instruments must be stated explicitly to examinees.

10. The member must proceed with caution when attempting to evaluate and interpret the performance of minority group members or other persons who are not represented in the norm group on which the instrument was standardized.

11. The member must guard against the appropriation, reproduction, or modifications of published tests or parts thereof without acknowledgment and permission from the previous publisher.

12. Regarding the preparation, publication and distribution of tests, reference should be made to:

a. *Standards for Educational and Psychological Tests and Manuals,* revised edition, 1974, published by the American Psychological Association on behalf of itself, the American Educational Research Association and the National Council on Measurement in Education.

b. The responsible use of tests: A position paper of AMEG, APGA, and NCME. *Measurement and Evaluation in Guidance,* 1972, 5, 385–388.

c. "Responsibilities of Users of Standardized Tests," APGA, *Guidepost,* October 5, 1978, pp. 5–8.

Section D—Research and Publication

1. Guidelines on research with human subjects shall be adhered to, such as:

a. *Ethical Principles in the Conduct of Research with Human Participants,* Washington, D.C.: American Psychological Association, Inc., 1973.

b. Code of Federal Regulations, Title 45, Subtitle A, Part 46, as currently issued.

2. In planning any research activity dealing with human subjects, the member must be aware of and responsive to all pertinent ethical principles and ensure that the research problem, design, and execution are in full compliance with them.

3. Responsibility for ethical research practice lies with the principal researcher, while others involved in the research activities share eithical obligation and full responsibility for their own actions.

4. In research with human subjects, researchers are responsible for the subjects' welfare throughout the experiment and they must take all reasonable precautions to avoid causing injurious psychological, physical, or social effects on their subjects.

5. All research subjects must be informed of the purpose of the study except when withholding information or providing misinformation to them is essential to the investigation. In such research the member must be responsi-

ble for corrective action as soon as possible following completion of the research.

6. Participation in research must be voluntary. Involuntary participation is appropriate only when it can be demonstrated that participation will have no harmful effects on subjects and is essential to the investigation.

7. When reporting research results, explicit mention must be made of all variables and conditions known to the investigator that might affect the outcome of the investigation or the interpretation of the data.

8. The member must be responsible for conducting and reporting investigations in a manner that minimizes the possibility that results will be misleading.

9. The member has an obligation to make available sufficient original research data to qualified others who may wish to replicate the study.

10. When supplying data, aiding in the research of another person, reporting research results, or in making original data available, due care must be taken to disguise the identity of the subjects in the absence of specific authorization from such subjects to do otherwise.

11. When conducting and reporting research, the member must be familiar with, and give recognition to, previous work on the topic, as well as to observe all copyright laws and follow the principles of giving full credit to all to whom credit is due.

12. The member must give due credit through joint authorship, acknowledgment, footnote statements, or other appropriate means to those who have contributed significantly to the research and/or publication, in accordance with such contributions.

13. The member must communicate to other members the results of any research judged to be of professional or scientific value. Results reflecting unfavorably on institutions, programs, services, or vested interests must not be withheld for such reasons.

14. If members agree to cooperate with another individual in research and/or publication, they incur an obligation to cooperate as promised in terms of punctuality of performance and with full regard to the completeness and accuracy of the information required.

15. Ethical practice requires that authors not submit the same manuscript or one essentially similar in content, for simultaneous publication consideration by two or more journals. In addition, manuscripts published in whole or in substantial part, in another journal or published wotk should not be submitted for publication without acknowledgment and permission from the previous publication.

Section E—Consulting

Consultation refers to a voluntary relationship between a professional helper and help-needing individual, group or social unit in which the consultant is providing help to the client(s) in defining and solving a work-related problem or potential problem with a client or client system. (This definition is adapted from Kurpius, DeWayne. Consultation theory and process: An integrated model. *Personnel and Guidance Journal,* 1978, 56.

1. The member acting as consultant must have a high degree of self-awareness of his-her own values, knowledge, skills, limitations, and needs in entering a helping relationship that involves human and-or organizational change and that the focus of the relationship be on the issues to be resolved and not on the person(s) presenting the problem.

2. There must be understanding and agreement between member and client for the problem definition, change goals, and predicated consequences of interventions selected.

3. The member must be reasonably certain that she/he or the organization represented has the necessary competencies and resources for giving the kind of help that is needed now or may develop later and that appropriate referral resources are available to the consultant.

4. The consulting relationship must be one in which client adaptability and growth toward self-direction are encouraged and cultivated. The member must maintain this role consistently and not become a decision maker for the client or create a future dependency on the consultant.

5. When announcing consultant availability for services, the member conscientiously adheres to the Association's *Ethical Standards.*

6. The member must refuse a private fee or other remuneration for consultation with persons who are entitled to the services through the member's employing institution or agency. The policies of a particular agency may make explicit provisions for private practice with agency clients by members of its staff. In such instances, the clients must be apprised of other options open to them should they seek private counseling services.

Section F—Private Practice

1. The member should assist the profession by facilitating the availability of counseling services in private as well as public settings.

2. In advertising services as a private practitioner, the member must advertise the services in such a manner so as to accurately inform the public as to services, expertise, profession, and techniques of counseling in a professional manner. A member who assumes an executive leadership role in the organization shall not permit his/her name to be used in professional notices during periods when not actively engaged in the private practice of counseling.

The member may list the following: highest relevant degree, type and level of certification or license, type and/or description of services, and other relevant information. Such information must not contain false, inaccurate, misleading, partial, out-of-context, or deceptive material or statements.

3. Members may join in partnership/corporation with other members and-or other professionals provided that each member of the partnership or cor-

poration makes clear the separate specialties by name in compliance with the regulations of the locality.

4. A member has an obligation to withdraw from a counseling relationship if it is believed that employment will result in violation of the *Ethical Standards*. If the mental or physical condition of the member renders it difficult to carry out an effective professional relationship or if the member is discharged by the client because the counseling relationship is no longer productive for the client, then the member is obligated to terminate the counseling relationship.

5. A member must adhere to the regulations for private practice of the locality where the services are offered.

6. It is unethical to use one's institutional affiliation to recruit clients for one's private practice.

Section G—Personnel Administration

It is recognized that most members are employed in public or quasi-public institutions. The functioning of a member within an institution must contribute to the goals of the institution and vice versa if either is to accomplish their respective goals or objectives. It is therefore essential that the member and the institution function in ways to (a) make the institution's goals explicit and public; (b) make the member's contribution to institutional goals specific; and (c) foster mutual accountability for goal achievement.

To accomplish these objectives, it is recognized that the member and the employer must share responsibilities in the formulation and implementation of personnel policies.

1. Members must define and describe the parameters and levels of their professional competency.

2. Members must establish interpersonal relations and working agreements with supervisors and subordinates regarding counseling or clinical relationships, confidentiality, distinction between public and private material, maintenance, and dissemination of recorded information, work load and accountability. Working agreements in each instance must be specified and made known to those concerned.

3. Members must alert their employers to conditions that may be potentially disruptive or damaging.

4. Members must inform employers of conditions that may limit their effectiveness.

5. Members must submit regularly to professional review and evaluation.

6. Members must be responsible for inservice development of self and-or staff.

7. Members must inform their staff of goals and programs.

8. Members must provide personnel practices that guarantee and enhance the rights and welfare of each recipient of their service.

9. Members must select competent persons and assign responsibilities compatible with their skills and experiences.

Section H—Preparation Standards

Members who are responsible for training others must be guided by the preparation standards of the Association and relevant Division(s). The member who functions in the capacity of trainer assumes unique ethical responsibilities that frequently go beyond that of the member who does not function in a training capacity. These ethical responsibilities are outlined as follows:

1. Members must orient students to program expectations, basic skills development, and employment prospects prior to admission to the program.
2. Members in charge of learning experiences must establish programs that integrate academic study and supervised practice.
3. Members must establish a program directed toward developing students' skills, knowledge, and self-understanding, stated whenever possible in competency or performance terms.
4. Members must identify the levels of competencies of their students in compliance with relevant Division standards. These competencies must accommodate the para-professional as well as the professional.
5. Members, through continual student evaluation and appraisal, must be aware of the personal limitations of the learner that might impede future performance. The instructor must not only assist the learner in securing remedial assistance but also screen from the program those individuals who are unable to provide competent services.
6. Members must provide a program that includes training in research commensurate with levels of role functioning. Para-professional and technician-level personnel must be trained as consumers of research. In addition, these personnel must learn how to evaluate their own and their program's effectiveness. Graduate training, especially at the doctoral level, would include preparation for original research by the member.
7. Members must make students aware of the ethical responsibilities and standards of the profession.
8. Preparatory programs must encourage students to value the ideals of service to individuals and to society. In this regard, direct financial remuneration or lack thereof must not influence the quality of service rendered. Monetary considerations must not be allowed to overshadow professional and humanitarian needs.
9. Members responsible for educational programs must be skilled as teachers and practitioners.
10. Members must present thoroughly varied theoretical positions so that students may make comparisons and have the opportunity to select a position.
11. Members must develop clear policies within their educational institutions regarding field placement and the roles of the student and the instructor in such placements.
12. Members must ensure that forms of learning focusing on self-understanding or growth are voluntary, of ir required as part of the education program, are made known to prospective students prior to entering the pro-

gram. When the education program offers a growth experience with an emphasis on self-disclosure or other relatively intimate or personal involvement, the member must have no administrative, supervisory, or evaluating authority regarding the participant.

13. Members must conduct an educational program in keeping with the current relevant guidelines of the American Personnel and Guidance Association and its Divisions.

Appendix C

Family Educational and Privacy Rights

§ 1232g. Family educational and privacy rights

(a) Conditions for availability of funds to educational agencies or institutions; inspection and review of education records; specific information to be made available; procedure for access to education records; reasonableness of time for such access; hearings; written explanations by parents; definitions. (1)(A) No funds shall be made available under any applicable program to any educational agency or institution which has a policy of denying, or which effectively prevents, the parents of students who are or have been in attendance at a school of such agency or at such institution, as the case may be, the right to inspect and review the education records of their children. If any material or document in the education record of a student includes information on more than one student, the parents of one of such students shall have the right to inspect and review only such part of such material or document as relates to such student or to be informed of the specific information contained in such part of such material. Each educational agency or institution shall establish appropriate procedures for the granting of a request by parents for access to the education records of their children within a reasonable period of

Reprinted from 20 USCS § § 1232g, 1232h

time, but in no case more than forty-five days after the request has been made.

(B) The first sentence of subparagraph (A) shall not operate to make available to students in institutions of postsecondary education the following materials:

(i) financial records of the parents of the student or any information contained therein;

(ii) confidential letters and statements of recommendation, which were placed in the education records prior to January 1, 1975, if such letters or statements are not used for purposes other than those for which they were specifically intended;

(iii) if the student has signed a waiver of the student's right of access under this subsection in accordance with subparagraph (C), confidential recommendations—

(I) respecting admission to any educational agency or institution,

(II) respecting an application for employment, and

(III) respecting the receipt of an honor or honorary recognition.

(C) A student or a person applying for admission may waive his right of access to confidential statements described in clause (iii) of subparagraph (B), except that such waiver shall apply to recommendations only if (i) the student is, upon request, notified of the names of all persons making confidential recommendations and (ii) such recommendations are used solely for the purpose for which they were specifically intended. Such waivers may not be required as a condition for admission to, receipt of financial aid from, or receipt of any other services or benefits from such agency or institution.

(2) No funds shall be made available under any applicable program to any educational agency or institution unless the parents of students who are or have been in attendance at a school of such agency or at such institution are provided an opportunity for a hearing by such agency or institution, in accordance with regulations of the Secretary, to challenge the content of such student's education records, in order to insure that the records are not inaccurate, misleading, or otherwise in violation of the privacy or other rights of students, and to provide an opportunity for the correction or deletion of any such inaccurate, misleading, or otherwise inappropriate data contained therein and to insert into such records a written explanation of the parents respecting the content of such records.

(3) For the purposes of this section the term "educational agency or institution" means any public or private agency or institution which is the recipient of funds under any applicable program.

(4)(A) For the purposes of this section, the term "education records" means, except as may be provided otherwise in subparagraph (B), those records, files, documents, and other materials which—

(i) contain information directly related to a student; and

(ii) are maintained by an educational agency or institution or by a person acting for such agency or institution.

(B) The term "education records" does not include—

(i) records of instructional, supervisory, and administrative personnel and educational personnel ancillary thereto which are in the sole possession of the maker thereof and which are not accessible or revealed to any other person except a substitute;

(ii) if the personnel of a law enforcement unit do not have access to education records under subsection (b)(1), the records and documents of such law enforcement unit which (I) are kept apart from records described in subparagraph (A), (II) are maintained solely for law enforcement purposes, and (III) are not made available to persons other than law enforcement officials of the same jurisdiction;

(iii) in the case of persons who are employed by an educational agency or institution but who are not in attendance at such agency or institution, records made and maintained in the normal course of business which relate exclusively to such person in that person's capacity as an employee and are not available for use for any other purpose; or

(iv) records on a student who is eighteen years of age or older, or is attending an institution of postsecondary education, which are made or maintained by a physician, psychiatrist, psychologist, or other recognized professional or paraprofessional acting in his professional or paraprofessional capacity, or assisting in that capacity, and which are made, maintained, or used only in connection with the provision of treatment to the student, and are not available to anyone other than persons providing such treatment, except that such records can be personally reviewed by a physician or other appropriate professional of the student's choice.

(5)(A) For the purposes of this section the term "directory information" relating to a student includes the following: the student's name, address, telephone listing, date and place of birth, major field of study, participation in officially recognized activities and sports, weight and height of members of athletic teams, dates of attendance, degrees and awards received, and the most recent previous educational agency or institution attended by the student.

(B) Any educational agency or institution making public directory information shall give public notice of the categories of information which it has designated as such information with respect to each student attending the institution or agency and shall allow a reasonable period of time after such notice has been given for a parent to inform the institution or agency that any or all of the information designated should not be released without the parent's prior consent.

(6) For the purposes of this section, the term "student" includes any person with respect to whom an educational agency or institution maintains education records or personally identifiable information, but does not include a person who has not been in attendance at such agency or institution.

(b) **Release of education records; parental consent requirement; exceptions; compliance with judicial orders and subpoenas; audit and evaluation of Federally-supported education programs; recordkeeping.** (1) No funds shall be made available under any applicable program to any educational agency or institution which has a policy or practice of permitting the release of educational records (or personally identifiable information contained therein other than directory information, as defined in paragraph (5) of subsection (a)) of students without the written consent of their parents to any individual, agency, or organization, other than to the following—

(A) other school officials, including teachers within the educational institution or local educational agency, who have been determined by such agency or institution to have legitimate educational interests;

(B) officials of other schools or school systems in which the student seeks or intends to enroll, upon condition that the student's parents be notified of the transfer, receive a copy of the record if desired, and have an opportunity for a hearing to challenge the content of the record;

(C) authorized representatives of (i) the Comptroller General of the United States, (ii) the Secretary, (iii) an administrative head of an educational agency (as defined in section 408(c) [20 USCS § 1221e-3(c)]), or (iv) State educational authorities, under the conditions set forth in paragraph (3) of this subsection;

(D) in connection with a student's application for, or receipt of, financial aid;

(E) State and local officials or authorities to whom such information is specifically required to be reported or disclosed pursuant to State statute adopted prior to November 19, 1974;

(F) organizations conducting studies for, or on behalf of, educational agencies or institutions for the purpose of developing, validating, or administering predictive tests, administering student aid programs, and improving instruction, if such studies are conducted in such a manner as will not permit the personal identification of students and their parents by persons other than representatives of such organizations and such information will be destroyed when no longer needed for the purpose for which it is conducted;

(G) accrediting organizations in order to carry out their accrediting functions;

(H) parents of a dependent student of such parents, as defined in section 152 of the Internal Revenue Code of 1954 [26 USCS § 152]; and

(I) subject to regulations of the Secretary, in connection with an emergency, appropriate persons if the knowledge of such information is necessary to protect the health or safety of the student or other persons.

Nothing in clause (E) of this paragraph shall prevent a State from further limiting the number or type of State or local officials who will continue to have access thereunder.

(2) No funds shall be made available under any applicable program to any educational agency or institution which has a policy or practice of releasing, or providing access to, any personally identifiable information in education records other than directory information, or as is permitted under paragraph (1) of this subsection unless—

(A) there is written consent from the student's parents specifying records to be released, the reasons for such release, and to whom, and with a copy of the records to be released to the student's parents and the student if desired by the parents, or

(B) such information is furnished in compliance with judicial order, or pursuant to any lawfully issued subpoena, upon condition that parents and the students are notified of all such orders or subpoenas in advance of the compliance therewith by the educational institution or agency.

(3) Nothing contained in this section shall preclude authorized representatives of (A) the Comptroller General of the United States, (B) the Secretary, (C) an administrative head of an education agency or (D) State educational authorities from having access to student or other records which may be necessary in connection with the audit and evaluation of Federally-supported education program, or in connection with the enforcement of the Federal legal requirements which relate to such programs: Provided, That except when collection of personally identifiable information is specifically authorized by Federal law, any data collected by such officials shall be protected in a manner which will not permit the personal identification of students and their parents by other than those officials, and such personally identifiable data shall be destroyed when no longer needed for such audit, evaluation, and enforcement of Federal legal requirements.

(4)(A) Each educational agency or institution shall maintain a record, kept with the education records of each student, which will indicate all individuals (other than those specified in paragraph (1)(A) of this subsection), agencies, or organizations which have requested or obtained access to a student's education records maintained by such educational agency or institution, and which will indicate specifically the legitimate interest that each such person, agency, or organization has in obtaining this information. Such record of access shall be available only to parents, to the school official and his assistants who are responsible for the custody of such records, and to persons or organizations authorized in, and under the conditions of, clauses (A) and (C) of paragraph (1) as a means of auditing the operation of the system.

(B) With respect to this subsection, personal information shall only be transferred to a third party on the condition that such party will not permit any other party to have access to such information without the written consent of the parents of the student.

(5) Nothing in this section shall be construed to prohibit State and local educational officials from having access to student or other records which may be necessary in connection with the audit and evaluation of any federally or State supported education program or in connection with the enforcement of the Federal legal requirements which relate to any such program, subject to the conditions specified in the proviso in paragraph (3).

(c) Surveys or data-gathering activities; regulations. The Secretary shall adopt appropriate regulations to protect the rights of privacy of students and their families in connection with any surveys or data-gathering activities conducted, assisted, or authorized by the Secretary or an administrative head of an education agency. Regulations established under this subsection shall include provisions controlling the use, dissemination, and protection of such data. No survey or data-gathering activities shall be conducted by the Secretary, or an administrative head of an education agency under an applicable program, unless such activities are authorized by law.

(d) Students' rather than parents' permission or consent. For the purposes of this section, whenever a student has attained eighteen years of age, or is attending an institution of postsecondary education the permission or consent required of and the rights accorded to the parents of the student shall thereafter only be required of and accorded to the student.

(e) Informing parents or students of rights under this section. No funds shall be made available under any applicable program to any educational agency or institution unless such agency or institution informs the parents of students, or the students, if they are eighteen years of age or older, or are attending an institution of postsecondary education, of the rights accorded them by this section.

(f) Enforcement; termination of assistance. The Secretary, or an administrative head of an education agency, shall take appropriate actions to enforce provisions of this section and to deal with violations of this section, according to the provisions of this Act, except that action to terminate assistance may be taken only if the Secretary finds there has been a failure to comply with the provisions of this section, and he has determined that compliance cannot be secured by voluntary means.

(g) Office and review board; creation; functions. The Secretary shall establish or designate an office and review board within the Department of Health, Education, and Welfare for the purpose of investigating, processing, reviewing, and adjudicating violations of the provisions of this section and complaints which may be filed concerning alleged violations of this section. Except for the conduct of hearings, none of the functions of the Secretary under this section shall be carried out in any of the regional offices of such Department.

(Jan. 2, 1968, P. L. 90-247, Title IV, Part C, Subpart 2, § 438, as added Aug. 21, 1974, P. L. 93-380, Title V, § 513(a), 88 Stat. 571; Dec. 31, 1974. P. L. 93-568, § 2(a), 88 Stat. 1858; Aug. 6, 1979, P. L. 96-46, § 4(c), 9. Stat. 342.)

§ 1232h. Protection of pupil rights

(a) Inspection by parents or guardians of instructional material. All instructional material, including teacher's manuals, films, tapes, or other supplementary instructional material which will be used in connection with any research or experimentation program or project shall be available for inspection by the parents or guardians of the children engaged in such program or project. For the purpose of this section "research or experimentation program or project" means any program or project in any applicable program designed to explore or develop new or unproven teaching methods or techniques.

(b) Psychiatric or psychological examinations, testing, or treatment. No student shall be required, as part of any applicable program, to submit to psychiatric examination, testing, or treatment, or psychological examination, testing, or treatment, in which the primary purpose is to reveal information concerning:

(1) political affiliations;

(2) mental and psychological problems potentially embarrassing to the student or his family;

(3) sex behavior and attitudes;

(4) illegal, anti-social, self-incriminating and demeaning behavior;

(5) critical appraisals of other individuals with whom respondents have close family relationships;

(6) legally recognized privileged and analogous relationships, such as those of lawyers, physicians, and ministers; or

(7) income (other than that required by law to determine eligibility for participation in a program or for receiving financial assistance under such program), without the prior consent of the student (if the student is an adult or emancipated minor), or in the case of unemancipated minor, without the prior written consent of the parent.

(Jan. 2, 1968, P. L. 90-247, Title IV, Part C, Subpart 2, § 439, as added Aug. 21, 1974, P. L. 93-380, Title V, § 514(a), 88 Stat. 574; Nov. 1, 1978, P. L. 95-561, Title XII, Part D, § 1250, 92 Stat. 2355.)

Appendix D

Rehabilitation Act of 1973

§ 794. Nondiscrimination under Federal grants and programs; promulgation of rules and regulations

No otherwise qualified handicapped individual in the United States, as defined in section 7(7) [29 USCS § 706(7)], shall, solely by reason of his handicap, be excluded from the participation in, be denied the benefits of, or be subjected to discrimination under any program or activity receiving Federal financial assistance or under any program or activity conducted by any Executive agency or by the United States Postal Service. The head of each such agency shall promulgate such regulations as may be necessary to carry out the amendments to this section made by the Rehabilitation, Comprehensive Services, and Developmental Disabilities Act of 1978. Copies of any proposed regulation shall be submitted to appropriate authorizing committees of the Congress, and such regulation may take effect no earlier than the thirtieth day after the date on which such regulation is so submitted to such committees.

(Sept. 26, 1973, P. L. 93-112, Title V, § 504, 87 Stat 394; Nov. 6, 1978, P. L. 95-602, Title I, §§ 119, 122(d)(2), 92 Stat. 2982, 2987.)

Reprinted from 29 USCS § 794

(7)(A) Except as otherwise provided in subparagraph (B), the term "handicapped individual" means any individual who (i) has a physical or mental disability which for such individual constitutes or results in a substantial handicap to employment and (ii) can reasonably be expected to benefit in terms of employability from vocational rehabilitation services provided pursuant to titles I and III of this Act [29 USCS §§ 720 et seq., 770 et seq.].

(B) Subject to the second sentence of this subparagraph, the term "handicapped individual" means, for purposes of titles IV and V of this Act [29 USCS §§ 780 et seq., 790 et seq.], any person who (i) has a physical or mental impairment which substantially limits one or more of such person's major life activities, (ii) has a record of such an impairment, or (iii) is regarded as having such an impairment. For purposes of sections 503 and 504 [29 USCS §§ 793, 794] as such sections relate to employment, such term does not include any individual who is an alcoholic or drug abuser whose current use of alcohol or drugs prevents such individual from performing the duties of the job in question or whose employment, by reason of such current alcohol or drug abuse, would constitute a direct threat to property or the safety of others.

Appendix E

Education of the Handicapped

§ 1401. Definitions

As used in this title—

(1) The term "handicapped children" means mentally retarded, hard of hearing, deaf, speech impaired, visually handicapped, seriously emotion-

Reprinted from 20 USCS § § 1401, 1415

ally disturbed, orthopedically impaired, or other health impaired children, or children with specific learning disabilities, who by reason thereof require special education and related services.

(2)[Omitted]

(3) The term "Advisory Committee" means the National Advisory Committee on Handicapped Children.

(4) The term "construction", except where otherwise specified, means (A) erection of new or expansion of existing structures, and the acquisition and installation of equipment therefor; or (B) acquisition of existing structures not owned by any agency or institution making application for assistance under this title; or (C) remodeling or alteration (including the acquisition, installation, modernization, or replacement of equipment) of existing structures; or (D) acquisition of land in connection with the activities in clauses (A), (B), and (C); or (E) a combination of any two or more of the foregoing.

(5) The term "equipment" includes machinery, utilities, and built-in equipment and any necessary enclosures or structures to house them, and includes all other items necessary for the functioning of a particular facility as a facility for the provision of educational services, including items such as instructional equipment and necessary furniture, printed, published, and audio-visual instructional materials, telecommunications, sensory, and other technological aids and devices, and books, periodicals, documents, and other related materials.

(6) The term "State" means each of the several States, the District of Columbia, the Commonwealth of Puerto Rico, Guam, American Samoa, the Virgin Islands and the Trust Territory of the Pacific Islands.

(7) The term "State educational agency" means the State board of education or other agency or officer primarily responsible for the State supervision of public elementary and secondary schools, or, if there is no such officer or agency, an officer or agency designated by the Governor or by State law.

(8) The term "local educational agency" means a public board of education or other public authority legally constituted within a State for either administrative control or direction of, or to perform a service function for, public elementary or secondary schools in a city, county, township, school district, or other political subdivision of a State, or such combination of school districts or counties as are recognized in a State as an administrative agency for its public elementary or secondary schools. Such term also includes any other public institution or agency having administrative control and direction of a public elementary or secondary school.

(9) The term "elementary school" means a day or residential school which provides elementary education, as determined under State law.

(10) The term "secondary school" means a day or residential school which provides secondary education, as determined under State law, except that it does not include any education provided beyond grade 12.

(11) The term "institution of higher education" means an educational institution in any State which—

(A) admits as regular students only individuals having a certificate of graduation from a high school, or the recognized equivalent of such a certificate;

(B) is legally authorized within such State to provide a program of education beyond high school;

(C) provides an educational program for which it awards a bachelor's degree, or provides not less than a two-year program which is acceptable for full credit toward such a degree, or offers a two-year program in engineering, mathematics, or the physical or biological sciences which is designed to prepare the student to work as a technician and at a semiprofessional level in engineering, scientific, or other technological fields which require the understanding and application of basic engineering, scientific, or mathematical principles or knowledge;

(D) is a public or other nonprofit institution; and

(E) is accredited by a nationally recognized accrediting agency or association listed by the Commissioner pursuant to this paragraph or, if not so accredited, is an institution whose credits are accepted, on transfer, by not less than three institutions which are so accredited, for credit on the same basis as if transferred from an institution so accredited: Provided, however, That in the case of an institution offering a two-year program in engineering, mathematics, or the physical or biological sciences which is designed to prepare the student to work as a technician and at a semiprofessional level in engineering, scientific, or technological fields which require the understanding and application of basic engineering, scientific, or mathematical principles or knowledge, if the Commissioner determines that there is no nationally recognized accrediting agency or association qualified to accredit such institutions, he shall appoint an advisory committee, composed of persons specially qualified to evaluate training provided by such institutions, which shall prescribe the standards of content, scope, and quality which must be met in order to qualify such institutions to participate under this Act and shall also determine whether particular institutions meet such standards. For the purposes of this paragraph the Commissioner shall publish a list of nationally recognized accrediting agencies or associations which he determines to be reliable authority as to the quality of education or training offered.

(12) The term "nonprofit" as applied to a school, agency, organization, or institution means a school, agency, organization, or institution owned and operated by one or more nonprofit corporations or associations no

part of the net earnings of which inures, or may lawfully inure, to the benefit of any private shareholder or individual.

(13) The term "research and related purposes" means research, research training (including the payment of stipends and allowances), surveys, or demonstrations in the field of education of handicapped children, or the dissemination of information derived therefrom, including (but without limitation) experimental schools.

(14) The term "Secretary" means the Secretary of Health, Education, and Welfare.

(15) The term "children with specific learning disabilities" means those children who have a disorder in one or more of the basic psychological processes involved in understanding or in using language, spoken or written, which disorder may manifest itself in imperfect ability to listen, think, speak, read, write, spell, or do mathematical calculations. Such disorders include such conditions as perceptual handicaps, brain injury, minimal brain dysfunction, dyslexia, and developmental aphasia. Such term does not include children who have learning problems which are primarily the result of visual, hearing, or motor handicaps, of mental retardation, of emotional disturbance, or of environmental, cultural, or economic disadvantage.

(16) The term "special education" means specially designed instruction, at no cost to parents or guardians, to meet the unique needs of a handicapped child, including classroom instruction, instruction in physical education, home instruction, and instruction in hospitals and institutions.

(17) The term "related services" means transportation, and such developmental, corrective, and other supportive services (including speech pathology and audiology, psychological services, physical and occupational therapy, recreation, and medical and counseling services, except that such medical services shall be for diagnostic and evaluation purposes only) as may be required to assist a handicapped child to benefit from special education, and includes the early identification and assessment of handicapping conditions in children.

(18) The term "free appropriate public education" means special education and related services which (A) have been provided at public expense, under public supervision and direction, and without charge, (B) meet the standards of the State educational agency, (C) include an appropriate preschool, elementary, or secondary school education in the State involved, and (D) are provided in conformity with the individualized education program required under section 614(a)(5) [20 USCS § 1414(a)(5)].

(19) The term "individualized education program" means a written statement for each handicapped child developed in any meeting by a representative of the local educational agency or an intermediate educational unit who shall be qualified to provide, or supervise the provision of, specially designed instruction to meet the unique needs of handi-

capped children, the teacher, the parents or guardian of such child, and, whenever appropriate, such child, which statement shall include (A) a statement of the present levels of educational performance of such child, (B) a statement of annual goals, including short-term instructional objectives, (C) a statement of the specific educational services to be provided to such child, and the extent to which such child will be able to participate in regular educational programs, (D) the projected date for initiation and anticipated duration of such services, and (E) appropriate objective criteria and evaluation procedures and schedules for determining, on at least an annual basis, whether instructional objectives are being achieved.

(20) The term "excess costs" means those costs which are in excess of the average annual per student expenditure in a local educational agency during the preceding school year for an elementary or secondary school student, as may be appropriate, and which shall be computed after deducting (A) amounts received under this part [20 USCS §§ 1400 et seq.] or under title I or title VII of the Elementary and Secondary Education Act of 1965, and (B) any State or local funds expended for programs which would qualify for assistance under this part [20 USCS §§ 1400 et seq.] or under such titles.

(21) The term "native language" has the meaning given that term by section 703(a)(2) of the Bilingual Education Act (20 U.S.C. 880b-1(a)(2)).

(22) The term "intermediate educational unit" means any public authority, other than a local educational agency, which is under the general supervision of a State educational agency, which is established by State law for the purpose of providing free public education on a regional basis, and which provides special education and related services to handicapped children within that State.

(Apr. 13, 1970, P. L. 91-230, Title VI, Part A, § 602, 84 Stat. 175; Nov. 29, 1975, P. L. 94-142, § 4(a), 89 Stat. 775.)

§ 1415. Procedural safeguards

(a) Establishment and maintenance. Any State educational agency, any local educational agency, and any intermediate educational unit which receives assistance under this part shall establish and maintain procedures in accordance with subsection (b) through subsection (e) of this section to assure that handicapped children and their parents or guardians are guaranteed procedural safeguards with respect to the provision of free appropriate public education by such agencies and units.

(b) Required procedures; hearing. (1) The procedures required by this section shall include, but shall not be limited to—

(A) an opportunity for the parents or guardian of a handicapped child to examine all relevant records with respect to the identification, evaluation, and educational placement of the child, and the provision of a free appropriate public education to such child, and to obtain an independent educational evaluation of the child;

(B) procedures to protect the rights of the child whenever the parents or guardian of the child are not known, unavailable, or the child is a ward of the State, including the assignment of an individual (who shall not be an employee of the State educational agency, local educational agency, or intermediate educational unit involved in the education or care of the child) to act as a surrogate for the parents or guardian;

(C) written prior notice to the parents or guardian of the child whenever such agency or unit—

(i) proposes to initiate or change, or

(ii) refuses to initiate or change,

the identification, evaluation, or educational placement of the child or the provision of a free appropriate public education to the child;

(D) procedures designed to assure that the notice required by clause (C) fully inform the parents or guardian, in the parents' or guardian's native language, unless it clearly is not feasible to do so, of all procedures available pursuant to this section; and

(E) an opportunity to present complaints with respect to any matter relating to the identification, evaluation, or educational placement of the child, or the provision of a free appropriate public education to such child.

(2) Whenever a complaint has been received under paragraph (1) of this subsection, the parents or guardian shall have an opportunity for an impartial due process hearing which shall be conducted by the State educational agency or by the local educational agency or intermediate educational unit, as determined by State law or by the State educational agency. No hearing conducted pursuant to the requirements of this paragraph shall be conducted by an employee of such agency or unit involved in the education or care of the child.

(c) Review of local decision by State educational agency. If the hearing required in paragraph (2) of subsection (b) of this section is conducted by a local educational agency or an intermediate educational unit, any party aggrieved by the findings and decision rendered in such a hearing may appeal to the State educational agency which shall conduct an impartial review of such hearing. The officer conducting such review shall make an independent decision upon completion of such review.

(d) Enumeration of rights accorded parties to hearings. Any party to any hearing conducted pursuant to subsections (b) and (c) shall be accorded (1) the right to be accompanied and advised by counsel and by individuals with special knowledge or training with respect to the problems of handicapped children, (2) the right to present evidence and confront, cross-examine, and compel the attendance of witnesses, (3) the right to a written or electronic verbatim record of such hearing, and (4) the right to written findings of fact and decisions (which findings and decisions shall also be transmitted to the advisory panel established pursuant to section 613(a)(12) [20 USCS § 1413(a)(12)]).

(e) Civil action; jurisdiction. (1) A decision made in a hearing conducted pursuant to paragraph (2) of subsection (b) shall be final, except that any party involved in such hearing may appeal such decision under the provisions of subsection (c) and paragraph (2) of this subsection. A decision made under subsection (c) shall be final, except that any party may bring an action under paragraph (2) of this subsection.

(2) Any party aggrieved by the findings and decision made under subsection (b) who does not have the right to an appeal under subsection (c), and any party aggrieved by the findings and decision under subsection (c), shall have the right to bring a civil action with respect to the complaint presented pursuant to this section, which action may be brought in any State court of competent jurisdiction or in a district court of the United States without regard to the amount in controversy.

In any action brought under this paragraph the court shall receive the records of the administrative proceedings, shall hear additional evidence at the request of a party, and, basing its decision on the preponderance of the evidence, shall grant such relief as the court determines is appropriate.

(3) During the pendency of any proceedings conducted pursuant to this section, unless the State or local educational agency and the parents or guardian otherwise agree, the child shall remain in the then current educational placement of such child, or, if applying for initial admission to a public school, shall, with the consent of the parents or guardian, be placed in the public school program until all such proceedings have been completed.

(4) The district courts of the United States shall have jurisdiction of actions brought under this subsection without regard to the amount in controversy.

(Apr. 13, 1970, P. L. 91-230, Title VI, Part B, § 615, as added Nov. 29, 1975, P. L. 94-142, § 5(a), 89 Stat. 788.)

Appendix F

Discrimination Based on Sex

§ 1681. Sex

(a) Prohibition against discrimination; exceptions. No person in the United States shall, on the basis of sex, be excluded from participation in, be denied the benefits of, or be subjected to discrimination under any education program or activity receiving Federal financial assistance, except that:

(1) Classes of educational institutions subject to prohibition. in regard to admissions to educational institutions, this section shall apply only to institutions of vocational education, professional education, and graduate higher education, and to public institutions of undergraduate higher education;

(2) Educational institutions commencing planned change in admissions. in regard to admissions to educational institutions, this section shall not

Reprinted from 20 USCS § 1681

apply (A) for one year from the date of enactment of this Act [enacted June 23, 1972], nor for six years after such date [June 23, 1972] in the case of an educational institution which has begun the process of changing from being an institution which admits only students of one sex to being an institution which admits students of both sexes, but only if it is carrying out a plan for such a change which is approved by the Commissioner of Education or (B) for seven years from the date an educational institution begins the process of changing from being an institution which admits only students of only one sex to being an institution which admits students of both sexes, but only if it is carrying out a plan for such a change which is approved by the Commissioner of Education, whichever is the later;

(3) Educational institutions of religious organizations with contrary religious tenets. this section shall not apply to an educational institution which is controlled by a religious organization if the application of this subsection would not be consistent with the religious tenets of such organization;

(4) Educational institutions training individuals for military services or merchant marine. this section shall not apply to an educational institution whose primary purpose is the training of individuals for the military services of the United States, or the merchant marine;

(5) Public educational institutions with traditional and continuing admissions policy. in regard to admissions this section shall not apply to any public institution of undergraduate higher education which is an institution that traditionally and continually from its establishment has had a policy of admitting only students of one sex;

(6) Social fraternities or sororities; voluntary youth service organizations. this section shall not apply to membership practices—

(A) of a social fraternity or social sorority which is exempt from taxation under section 501(a) of the Internal Revenue Code of 1954 [26 USCS § 501(a)], the active membership of which consists primarily of students in attendance at an institution of higher education, or

(B) of the Young Men's Christian Association, Young Women's Christian Association, Girl Scouts, Boy Scouts, Camp Fire Girls, and voluntary youth service organizations which are so exempt, the membership of which has traditionally been limited to persons of one sex and principally to persons of less than nineteen years of age;

(7) Boy or Girl conferences. this section shall not apply to—

(A) any program or activity of the American Legion undertaken in connection with the organization or operation of any Boys State conference, Boys Nation conference, Girls State conference, or Girls Nation conference; or

(B) any program or activity of any secondary school or educational institution specifically for—

(i) the promotion of any Boys State conference, Boys Nation conference, Girls State conference, or Girls Nation conference; or

(ii) the selection of students to attend any such conference;

(8) Father-son or mother-daughter activities at educational institutions. this section shall not preclude father-son or mother-daughter activities at an educational institution, but if such activities are provided for students of one sex, opportunities for reasonably comparable activities shall be provided for students of the other sex; and

(9) Institution of higher education scholarship awards in "beauty" pageants. this section shall not apply with respect to any scholarship or other financial assistance awarded by an institution of higher education to any individual because such individual has received such award in any pageant in which the attainment of such award is based upon a combination of factors related to the personal appearance, poise, and talent of such individual and in which participation is limited to individuals of one sex only, so long as such pageant is in compliance with other nondiscrimination provisions of Federal law.

(b) Preferential or disparate treatment because of imbalance in participation or receipt of Federal benefits; statistical evidence of imbalance. Nothing contained in subsection (a) of this section shall be interpreted to require any educational institution to grant preferential or disparate treatment to the members of one sex on account of an imbalance which may exist with respect to the total number or percentage of persons of that sex participating in or receiving the benefits of any federally supported program or activity, in comparison with the total number or percentage of persons of that sex in any community, State, section, or other area: Provided, That this subsection shall not be construed to prevent the consideration in any hearing or proceeding under this title of statistical evidence tending to show that such an imbalance exists with respect to the participation in, or receipt of the benefits of, any such program or activity by the members of one sex.

(c) Educational institution defined. For purposes of this title an educational institution means any public or private preschool, elementary, or secondary school, or any institution of vocational, professional, or higher education, except that in the case of an educational institution composed of more than one school, college, or department which are administratively separate units, such term means each such school, college, or department.

(June 23, 1972, P. L. 92-318, Title IX, § 901, 86 Stat. 373; Dec. 31, 1974, P. L. 93-568, § 3(a), 88 Stat. 1862; Oct. 12, 1976, P. L. 94-482, Title IV, § 412(a), 90 Stat. 2234.)

Appendix G

Child Abuse Prevention and Treatment

5101. National Center on Child Abuse and Neglect

Establishment. The Secretary of Health, Education, and Welfare [Secretary of Health and Human Services] (hereinafter referred to in this Act [42 USCS §§ 5101 et seq.] as the "Secretary") shall establish an office to be known as the National Center on Child Abuse and Neglect (hereinafter referred to in this Act [42 USCS §§ 5101 et seq.] as the "Center").

Functions. The Secretary, through the Center, shall—

(1) Annual research summary. compile, analyze, publish, and disseminate a summary annually of recently conducted and currently conducted research on child abuse and neglect;

(2) Information clearinghouse. develop and maintain an information clearinghouse on all programs, including private programs, showing promise of success, for the prevention, identification, and treatment of child abuse and neglect;

(3) Training materials for personnel. compile publish, and disseminate training materials for personnel who are engaged or intend to engage in the prevention, identification, and treatment of child abuse and neglect;

(4) Technical assistance. provide technical assistance (directly or through grant or contract) to public and nonprofit private agencies and organizations to assist them in planning, improving, developing, and carrying out programs and activities relating to the prevention, identification, and treatment of child abuse and neglect;

Reprinted from 42 USCS § § 5101, 5102, 5103, 5105, 5106

(5) Research into causes, prevention, identification, and treatmen conduct research into the causes of child abuse and neglect, and into th prevention, identification, and treatment thereof;

(6) Study. make a complete and full study and investigation of th national incidence of child abuse and neglect, including a determinatio of the extent to which incidents of child abuse and neglect are increasin in number or severity; and

(7) Plan. in consultation with Federal agencies serving on the Advisor Board on Child Abuse and Neglect (established by section 6 of this Ac [42 USCS § 5105], prepare a comprehensive plan for seeking to brin about maximum coordination of the goals, objectives, and activities c all agencies and organizations which have responsibilities for program and activities related to child abuse and neglect, and submit such plan t such Advisory Board not later than twelve months after the date c enactment of this clause [enacted Apr. 24, 1978].

The Secretary shall establish research priorities for making grants c contracts under clause (5) of this subsection and, not less than sixty day before establishing such priorities, shall publish in the Federal Register fc public comment a statement of such proposed priorities.

(c) Grant and contract authority. The Secretary may carry out his fun tions under subsection (b) of this section either directly or by way of gra or contract. Grants may be made under subsection (b)(5) for periods of n more than three years. Any such grant shall be reviewed at least annual by the Secretary, utilizing peer review mechanisms to assure the quali and progress of research conducted under such grant.

(d) Staff and resource availability to Center. The Secretary shall mak available to the Center such staff and resources as are necessary for th Center to carry out effectively its functions under this Act [42 USC §§ 5101 et seq.].

(Jan. 31, 1974, P. L. 93-247, § 2, 88 Stat. 5; Jan. 4, 1975, P. L. 93-64 § 8(d)(1), 88 Stat. 2310; Apr. 24, 1978, P. L. 95-266, Title I, § 101, 92 Sta 205.)

5102. Definition

or purposes of this Act [42 USCS §§ 5101 et seq.] the term "child abuse d neglect" means the physical or mental injury, sexual abuse or exploita- on, negligent treatment, or maltreatment of a child under the age of ghteen, or the age specified by the child protection law of the State in estion, by a person who is responsible for the child's welfare under cumstances which indicate that the child's health or welfare is harmed threatened thereby, as determined in accordance with regulations escribed by the Secretary.

an. 31, 1974, P. L. 93-247, § 3, 88 Stat. 5 Apr. 24, 1978, P. L. 95-266, tle I, § 102, 92 Stat. 206.)

5103. Demonstration or service programs and projects

Grants and contracts; scope of activities. The Secretary, through the enter, is authorized to make grants to, and enter into contracts with, blic agencies or nonprofit private organizations (or combinations thereof) r demonstration or service programs and projects designed to prevent, entify, and treat child abuse and neglect. Grants or contracts under this bsection may be—

(1) for the training programs for professional and paraprofessional personnel in the fields of medicine, law, education, social work, and other relevant fields who are engaged in, or intend to work in, the field of the prevention, identification, and treatment of child abuse and neglect; and training programs for children, and for persons responsible for the welfare of children, in methods of protecting children from child abuse and neglect;

(2) for the establishment and maintenance of centers, serving defined geographic areas, staffed by multidisciplinary teams of personnel trained in the prevention, identification, and treatment of child abuse and neglect cases, to provide a board range of services related to child abuse and neglect, including direct support and supervision of satellite centers and attention homes, as well as providing advice and consultation to individuals, agencies, and organizations which request such services;

(3) for furnishing services of teams of professional and paraprofessional personnel who are trained in the prevention, identification, and treatment of child abuse and neglect cases, on a consulting basis to small communities where such services are not available; and

(4) for such other innovative programs and projects, including programs and projects for parent self-help, and for prevention and treatment of drug-related child abuse and neglect, that show promise of successfully preventing or treating cases of child abuse and neglect as the Secretary may approve.

(b) Grants to States; qualifications for assistance; reduction of awar compliance of social security provisions with certain requirements. The Secretary, through the Center, is authorized to make grants to States for the purpose of assisting the States in developing, strength ing, and carrying out child abuse and neglect prevention and treatm programs.

(2) In order for a State to qualify for assistance under this subsecti such State shall—

(A) have in effect a State child abuse and neglect law which sh include provisions for immunity for persons reporting instances child abuse and neglect from prosecution, under any State or lo law, arising out of such reporting;

(B) provide for the reporting of known and suspected instances child abuse and neglect;

(C) provide that upon receipt of a report of known or suspec instances of child abuse or neglect an investigation shall be initia promptly to substantiate the accuracy of the report, and, upon finding of abuse or neglect, immediate steps shall be taken to prot the health and welfare of the abused or neglected child, as well that of any other child under the same care who may be in danger abuse or neglect;

(D) demonstrate that there are in effect throughout the State, connection with the enforcement of child abuse and neglect laws a with the reporting of suspected instances of child abuse and negle such administrative procedures, such personnel trained in child ab and neglect prevention and treatment, such training procedures, su institutional and other facilities (public and private), and such rela multidisciplinary programs and services as may be necessary appropriate to assure that the State will deal effectively with ch abuse and neglect cases in the State;

(E) provide for methods to preserve the confidentiality of all reco in order to protect the rights of the child, his parents or guardians;

(F) provide for the cooperation of law enforcement officials, courts competent jurisdiction, and appropriate State agencies providing h man services;

(G) provide that in every case involving an abused or neglected ch which results in a judicial proceeding a guardian ad litem shall appointed to represent the child in such proceedings;

(H) provide that the aggregate of support for programs or proje related to child abuse and neglect assisted by State funds shall not reduced below the level provided during fiscal year 1973, and set fo policies and procedures designed to assure that Federal funds ma available under this Act [42 USCS §§ 5101 et seq.] for any fiscal y will be so used as to supplement and, to the extent practical increase the level of State funds which would, in the absence Federal funds, be available for such programs and projects;

(I) provide for dissemination of information to the general public with respect to the problem of child abuse and neglect and the facilities and prevention and treatment methods available to combat instances of child abuse and neglect; and

(J) to the extent feasible, insure that parental organizations combating child abuse and neglect receive preferential treatment.

If a State has failed to obligate funds awarded under this subsection within eighteen months after the date of award, the next award under this subsection made after the expiration of such period shall be reduced by an amount equal to the amount of such unobligated funds unless the Secretary determines that extraordinary reasons justify the failure to so obligate.

(3) Programs or projects related to child abuse and neglect assisted under part A or B of title IV of the Social Security Act [42 USCS §§ 601 et seq. or 42 USCS §§ 620 et seq.] shall comply with the requirements set forth in clauses (B), (C), (E), and (F) of paragraph (2).

Prohibition of assistance for construction of facilities; lease or rental l alteration or repair of facilities. Assistance provided pursuant to this tion shall not be available for construction of facilities; however, the retary is authorized to supply such assistance for the lease or rental of ilities where adequate facilities are not otherwise available, and for air or minor remodeling or alteration of existing facilities.

Criteria for equitable distribution of assistance. The Secretary shall ablish criteria designed to achieve equitable distribution of assistance der this section among the States, among geographic areas of the tion, and among rural and urban areas. To the extent possible, citizens each State shall receive assistance from at least one project under this tion.

Definition. For the purpose of this section, the term "State" includes h of the several States, the District of Columbia, the Commonwealth of erto Rico, American Samoa, the Virgin Islands, Guam and the Trust rritories of the Pacific.

n. 31, 1974, P. L. 93-247, § 4, 88 Stat. 5; Jan. 4, 1975, P. L. 93-644, (d)(2), 88 Stat. 2310; Apr. 24, 1978, P. L. 95-266, Title I, § 103, 92 Stat. 5.)

5105. Advisory Board on Child Abuse and Neglect

Appointment; membership; representation from Federal agencies and eral public; functions. The Secretary shall, within sixty days after the te of enactment of this Act [enacted Jan. 31, 1974] appoint an Advisory ard on Child Abuse and Neglect (hereinafter referred to as the "Advisory Board"), which shall be composed of representatives from Fede agencies with responsibility for programs and activities related to ch abuse and neglect, including the Office of Child Development, the Office Education, the National Institute of Education, the National Institute Mental Health, the National Institute of Child Health and Human Dev opment, the Social and Rehabilitation Service, and the Health Servi Administration, and not less than three members from the general pub with experience or expertise in the field of child abuse and neglect. T Advisory Board shall assist the Secretary in coordinating programs a activities related to child abuse and neglect planned, administered, assisted under this Act [42 USCS §§ 5101 et seq.] with such programs a activities planned, administered, or assisted by the Federal agencies wh representatives are members of the Advisory Board. The Advisory Bo shall also assist the Secretary in the development of Federal standards child abuse and neglect prevention and treatment programs and projects.

(b) Review and submission of plan to President and Congress. T Advisory Board shall review the comprehensive plan submitted to it by Center pursuant to section 2(b)(7) [42 USCS § 5101(b)(7)], make su changes as it deems appropriate, and submit to the President and Congress a final such plan not later than eighteen months after the effect date of this subsection [enacted Apr. 24, 1978].

§ 5106. Coordination

The Secretary shall promulgate regulations and make such arrangements may be necessary or appropriate to ensure that there is effective coordi tion between programs related to child abuse and neglect under this A [42 USCS §§ 5101 et seq.] and other such programs which are assisted Federal funds.

(Jan. 31, 1974, P. L. 93-247, § 7, 88 Stat. 8.)

Glossary

certification The process whereby the department of education or other regulatory agency grants a document to persons meeting certain minimum skills required for a profession or occupation. This text refers to guidance counselors who must be certified by state departments of education.

certiorari "(To be more fully informed) an original writ or action whereby a cause is removed from an inferior to a superior court for trial" (Alexander, Corns, and McCann, 1969, 717).

civil action "An action which has for its object the recovery of private or civil rights, or compensation for their infraction" (Alexander, Corns, and McCann, 1969, 718).

common law A body of law that originates from customs and rulings of the court rather than from laws created by the legislatures (Black, 1968, 345-356).

confidentiality An ethical decision by the counselor not to reveal information obtained during the counseling interview.

constitutional right Rights guaranteed individuals by the Constitution that may not be limited by legislative action (Black, 1968, 385).

contract A written or verbal agreement between two or more parties that is enforceable in court.

contributory negligence Negligence by a person that contributes to injury and thus normally prevents recovery of damages.

counseling A professional relationship between a client and professional designed to bring about behavioral change in the client.

defendant The party against whom charges are filed or the person who must answer the charges (Alexander, Corns, and McCann, 1969, 719).

defamation Slander or libel directed toward another's reputation, thereby injuring another person's reputation or character by spoken words or in writing.

discrimination An act of special treatment or affording or denying privileges to a special group because of their culture, handicap, nationality, race, or sex.

double jeopardy Prosecuting a person or group a second time for the same offense (prohibited by the Fifth Amendment of the United States Constitution).

duress Pressure or coercion resulting in action or nonaction against a person's will through force, fear or persuasion.

ethical standards "A guide to proper professional practice" (Callis, 1976, 5).

expert witness A person qualified by experience, training, and knowledge who is accepted by the courts to testify as to facts and who may be requested to give his or her opinion regarding facts in his or her field of acknowledged area of expertise.

fundamental right Right(s) established by the United States Constitution and its amendments, such as freedom of speech, assembly, liberty, and/or freedom from or threat of unwarranted searches and seizures.

guidance The total services and responsibilities rendered by the counselor. Tolbert (1974) included "counseling—individual and group, group guidance and orientation, testing and assessment, information (occupational, educational, social and personal), consultation with parents, teachers and pupils, in-service education, placement, research and evaluation" within guidance (p. 204).

hearing A proceeding or a trial, generally public, during which sides present facts and arguments to a judge, hearing officer, or authorized panel, for a decision on the issues of fact(s) or law(s).

hearsay Second-hand testimony given by a person; that is, evidence based upon what a person has heard from another rather than upon personal knowledge (generally considered unreliable and usually inadmissable to record).

injunction A judicial order requiring the person to whom it is addressed to refrain from a particular action (Black, 1968, 923).

in loco parentis A person who stands in place of a parent and who has the rights and responsibility normally given to parents.

libel and slander The terms refer to the defamation of another's reputation by word of mouth, gestures, or writings. Slander is communicated by spoken word and libel by written word.

licensing A means of regulating the practice of a profession and/or title wherein the individual proves certain competencies by examination and/or other requirements.

malpractice Harm to another resulting from negligence. For example, when professionals fail to follow acceptable standards, damage may occur.

minor A person under a certain age defined by individual state laws. A minor is often defined as a person under 18 years of age.

negligence "A departure from usual practice; that is acceptable standards were not followed and due care was not exercised" (Van Hoose and Kottler, 1978, 97).

perjury Knowingly giving, under oath, false testimony.

plaintiff The party who brings the charges or files the complaint (Alexander, Corns, and McCann, 1969, 721).

police power of the state The power "to enact laws for the comfort, health, and prosperity of the state" (Alexander, 1976, 226).

privileged communication The legal right granted to certain professionals excusing them from testifying in a court of law.

public school counselor A professional counselor who is employed in a publicly owned and operated school as opposed to a private school or other work settings.

remand a case Alexander, Corns, and McCann defined this phrase as "an action by an appellate court to send the case base to the court from which it came for further proceeding there" (p. 722).

slander *See* libel.

statute A written law enacted by the legislature, "solemnly expressed according to the forms necessary to constitute it to the law of the state" (Black, 1968, 1581).

tort A legal injury or wrong against another, independent of contract (Alexander, Corns, and McCann, 1969, 723).

writ An order issued by a court of law directing an officer of the law to perform an act.

REFERENCES

Alexander, David, 1979, Legal issues in guidance, in *School Guidance Services,* T. H. Hohenshil and J. H. Miles, eds., Kendal/Hunt, Iowa, pp. 219-246.

Alexander, K., R. Corns, and W. McCann, 1969, *Public School Law,* West, St. Paul, Minn.

Black, H. C., 1968, *Black's Law Dictionary,* rev. 4th ed., West, St. Paul, Minn.

Callis, R., ed., 1976, *Ethical Standards Casebook,* 2nd ed., APGA Publications, Washington, D.C.

Tolbert, E. L., 1974, *Counseling for Career Development,* Houghton Mifflin, Boston.

Van Hoose, W. H., and J. Kottler, 1978, *Ethical and Legal Issues in Counseling and Psychotherapy,* Jossey-Bass, San Francisco.

INDEX